T0328677

Cambridge Elements ≣

Elements in Metaphysics
edited by
Tuomas E. Tahko
University of Bristol

PERSISTENCE

Kristie Miller
The University of Sydney

CAMBRIDGE
UNIVERSITY PRESS

University Printing House, Cambridge CB2 8BS, United Kingdom

One Liberty Plaza, 20th Floor, New York, NY 10006, USA

477 Williamstown Road, Port Melbourne, VIC 3207, Australia

314–321, 3rd Floor, Plot 3, Splendor Forum, Jasola District Centre,
New Delhi – 110025, India

103 Penang Road, #05–06/07, Visioncrest Commercial, Singapore 238467

Cambridge University Press is part of the University of Cambridge.

It furthers the University's mission by disseminating knowledge in the pursuit of education, learning, and research at the highest international levels of excellence.

www.cambridge.org
Information on this title: www.cambridge.org/9781009056007
DOI: 10.1017/9781009057356

First published 2022

A catalogue record for this publication is available from the British Library.

ISBN 978-1-009-05600-7 Paperback
ISSN 2633-9862 (online)
ISSN 2633-9854 (print)

Persistence

Elements in Metaphysics

DOI: 10.1017/9781009057356
First published online: August 2022

Kristie Miller
The University of Sydney

Author for correspondence: Kristie Miller, kristie.miller@sydney.edu.au

Abstract: Persistence realism is the view that ordinary sentences that we think and utter about persisting objects are often true. It involves both a semantic claim about what it would take for those sentences to be true and an ontological claim about the way things are. According to persistence realism, given what it would take for persistence sentences to be true, and given the ontology of our world, such sentences are often true. According to persistence error theory, they are not. This Element considers several different views about the conditions under which those sentences are true. It argues for a view on which it is relatively easy to vindicate persistence realism, because all it takes is for the world to be the way it seems to us. Thereby, it argues for the view that relations of numerical identity, or of being-part-of-the-same-object, are neither necessary nor sufficient for persistence realism.

Keywords: persistence, time, objects, realism, change

ISBNs: 9781009056007 (PB), 9781009057356 (OC)
ISSNs: 2633-9862 (online), 2633-9854 (print)

Contents

1 Introduction

'Yesterday I went to the grocery store and bought vegetables and tofu. I also purchased some kangaroo steak for Annie (a labradoodle), plus some self-raising flour. Annie turns ten in seven days. I can hardly believe it. It seems like only yesterday that she came home as a little black ball of fluff. Boy has she changed. Tomorrow I'll use the excess lemons that I picked from the lemon tree last week to make a lemon pudding using the flour. I'd like to be able to say, in two weeks' time, that we've used all those lemons. I can't imagine that the kangaroo steaks will last Annie any more than four days, so I'll need to go and buy more meat within the week. Still, at least I know I can give chicken a miss, since we discovered last year that Annie is allergic to a protein in chicken, and it's been giving her tummy problems for some years.'

Apart from being surprised (if you are) that some dogs are allergic to proteins in some meats, the above description probably strikes you as pretty mundane. It's the sort of thing any of us might write, utter, or think. The paragraph contains a lot of *persistence sentences*. These are sentences such as 'Annie turns ten in seven days', 'yesterday I went to the grocery store', 'tomorrow I'll use the excess lemons', and 'eating chicken has given Annie tummy problems for years'. Roughly speaking, persistence sentences are, or at least appear to be, about *persisting things*,[1] things that in some sense or other exist through time, or exist at different times, or as we say, *persist*.

We all utter persistence sentences. In fact, we utter them a lot. We also think *persistence thoughts*; these are the thoughts we have whose content is the content of persistence sentences. So, when I think to myself that I really must use the lemons that I picked last week, I think a persistence thought, and when I utter that sentence I utter a persistence sentence.

Let's say that if one thinks persistence thoughts or utters persistence sentences one is engaging in *persistence discourse*.

We engage in persistence discourse both inside and outside the philosophy room, and that discourse is important in a variety of different ways.

Consider, for instance, the question of whether this person, sitting in front of us, should be held responsible for assaulting James yesterday. A natural thought is that this person should only be held responsible for assaulting James yesterday if this person is the same person as the person who assaulted James yesterday. So, the person who is sitting in front of us here is responsible for assaulting James yesterday only if this person existed yesterday and did the assault. So, the truth of a sentence about moral responsibility, such as 'this person should be punished for assaulting James yesterday', seems to depend on

---

[1] I will use 'thing' as neutral between the various kinds of things that might be thought to persist.

the truth of certain persistence sentences such as 'this person existed yesterday and assaulted James'. Thus, which sentences about moral responsibility are true seems intimately connected to which persistence sentences are true.

Or, suppose we tell the person sitting in front of us that tomorrow someone will have to undergo a very painful procedure. Should the person sitting in front of us be frightened by this news? Should they anticipate the painful procedure? Well, it seems they should only if the person who will tomorrow undergo the procedure will be *them*. They should anticipate the procedure only if they will persist and be the person who undergoes the procedure. Or indeed, consider cases in which you are deliberating about what to do. Will you study tonight or go out for pizza? Will you buy that new car or put money away in savings? The very process of reasoning about what to do seems to assume that you will exist at later times: that there will be someone who is you, who will get to eat the pizza or use the savings. Thus, which sentences about practical rationality and prudence are true seems intimately connected to which persistence sentences are true.

By our very natures we seem to be creatures who are extended in time. We have lives with a beginning, middle, and end. You, now, seem to be the product of all that has gone before, and you, later, will surely be the product of your current choices. We all interact in the world in a way that presupposes that both we and the ordinary objects around us are extended in time. We assume that when we drive to work in our car it is the same car we are driving throughout the journey and that when we get home at the end of the day it will be the same labradoodle that greets us as the labradoodle that we earlier farewelled.

Our days are filled with persistence thoughts and these thoughts structure much of our way of being in the world. They structure the way we engage with others and the ways we reason about and think about ourselves. They structure our views about the ethical realm as well as our views about the prudential realm.

Sometimes persistence thoughts/sentences are about events and sometimes they are about objects. For instance, 'the concert went on for two hours' is a persistence sentence about an event, the concert. 'Annie was much smaller when she was a puppy' is about an object, Annie. While there are many interesting issues about the persistence of events, in this Element I focus predominantly on the persistence of objects and on persistence sentences about such objects.

There are several approaches we might take to persistence sentences. We might be *persistence realists*. *Persistence realism*, as I understand it, is the view that persistence sentences are truth-apt – they take a truth value – and often those sentences are true. So persistence realism entails that our persistence discourse is often true. We are not *systematically* thinking false persistence thoughts or uttering false persistence sentences. On this way of conceiving of persistence realism, it is not sufficient for persistence realism to be true that there are some persisting objects; it needs to be that those persisting objects often make true the persistence sentences we utter and the persistence thoughts we think.

An alternative to persistence realism is *persistence error theory*, according to which persistence sentences and persistence thoughts are truth-apt and are systematically false. Thus, if what we are doing in engaging in persistence discourse is asserting the content of those sentences, then our persistence discourse is systematically false. (I return to consider the connection between persistence discourse and persistence sentences in Section 3.)

On the face of it, persistence error theory might seem like a crazy view. Surely it's just *obvious* that, often, we utter true persistence sentences. Although persistence error theory is often ignored, in this Element I try to motivate the view. While I think that persistence realism is true, I don't think it is as obvious that it is true as has often been assumed. I think we need to argue in favour of persistence realism and that is what I aim to do in what follows.

One advantage of thinking about questions regarding persistence through the lenses of persistence realism and persistence error theory is that it forces us to clearly distinguish two questions. The first of these is the question: 'under what conditions are persistence sentences true?'. That is, which ways could our world be such that persistence sentences are true?

This question is different from another we want to ask: namely, 'how do actual objects persist?'. That is, assuming that persistence realism is true, and there are persisting objects, *how* do those objects persist? In the remainder of this Element I clearly demarcate these two questions and present a number of different answers to each of them.

Historically, philosophers have tended to focus predominantly on the second question or, at least, they are often interpreted as doing so. That is because it is often thought that the first question has an easy answer. What is it for an object to persist? Well, it's for that object to exist at multiple times.[2] So if there are the right sorts of objects that exist at different times, then often the persistence sentences that we take to be true will indeed be true. Since there are such objects, these sentences are indeed true. That being so, the only interesting question is *how it is* that objects exist at multiple times.

Conceived of in this way, the various views about persistence, provide competing accounts of the way in which actual objects persist. On this way of

---

[2] Lewis (1986, p. 202), for instance, describes persistence in this manner.

framing the contemporary debate, there is broad agreement about *what it is* for objects to persist – namely, to exist at multiple times – but disagreement about *how it is* that objects in fact persist.

There is clearly *something* right about the idea that what it is for something to persist is for it to (in some sense or other) exist at multiple times. Indeed, I think we can, and should, take this idea as a certain sort of 'subject setting' description. How do philosophers know they are all talking about the same sort of thing – persistence – and disagreeing about how it is that objects persist, rather than talking about different things altogether? Well, we know they are all talking about the same phenomenon because they all agree that, at some very broad level, what it is to persist is to exist at multiple times.

Still, I think that setting aside the question of what persistence is, and focussing only on the question of how objects persist, is a mistake; and it's a mistake even though we can all agree that persisting objects are objects that exist at multiple times. That is because if this is all we can say, then we haven't said anything very substantive. If what it is to persist is to exist at multiple times, then this advances our understanding of what persistence is only if we have a firm grasp on what it is to exist at multiple times. But we don't. We have roughly the same grasp on the idea of something existing at multiple times as we do on the idea of persistence itself. And that is why we need to say more about how to answer the first question: the question that requires that we spell out the ways our world can be such that persistence sentences are true (or not).

Moreover, if philosophers really did think that the question of what persistence is has already been answered, we'd expect them to agree that the various competitor views are all perfectly good accounts *of persistence*. We'd expect them to agree that objects might persist in this way and simply to disagree about whether they do.

Sometimes, however, something more seems to be going on in debates about persistence. Sometimes philosophers seem to think that if our world were as described by their opponents, then it wouldn't *really* be true that objects persist. These philosophers don't think that their opponents are offering false theories of how objects in fact are. Rather, they are better described as thinking that their opponents are offering a theory on which, properly understood, objects do not really persist at all. Or, to put the point back into the language of persistence realism and error theory, they think their opponents are offering views which, if true, would make persistence error theory true.

To capture this kind of disagreement we need to examine different potential answers to the first question: 'what is persistence?'. To do this, we can agree that at one level of abstraction what it is to persist is to exist at multiple times, while noting that this doesn't yet fully answer our question since we don't know *what it is to exist at multiple times*. Hence, a good deal of this Element will focus on different answers to the question, '*what* is persistence?', alongside the further, second question, '*how* do objects in fact persist?'. In doing so, I take a somewhat different approach to that often taken, which focusses predominantly on this second question. Hopefully, however, this approach will prove illuminating in several ways.

With this in mind, I begin, in Section 2, by articulating several answers to the question 'what is persistence?' by considering competing answers to the question, 'under what conditions are persistence sentences true?'. Then, in Section 3, I consider two arguments against persistence error theory. I explain why I think these arguments are bad and hence why I think we should take the view more seriously than we do. This is not to say that I defend persistence error theory. Far from it. In Sections 4, 5, and 6 I argue in favour of my preferred answer to the question, 'under what conditions are persistence sentences true?'. The answer I give is the view I call semantic processionism. Section 4 offers several arguments in favour of semantic processionism. Section 5 considers objections to the view and responds to these. Section 6 returns us to a consideration of persistence realism. There, I argue that one major virtue of semantic processionism is that it makes it very easy to vindicate persistence realism. If our world is, roughly, the way it seems to us to be, then it doesn't matter what underlying metaphysical nature it has; most of the persistence sentences that we take to be true will be true. Since this is not the case for competitor views, this is a good reason to endorse this view. Finally, in Section 7, I take up the question of how actual objects persist. My aim, in structuring things in this way, is to clearly differentiate arguments that target the first question from those that target the second question, and to clearly differentiate answers to the first question from answers to the second.

2 What Is Persistence?

Very few, if any, introductory texts on persistence would begin by discussing persistence realism and persistence error theory. In this Element I want to take seriously the idea that we should think more carefully about what persistence *itself* is. To do that, I will focus first on articulating persistence realism and persistence error theory (Section 2.1) before I present several views about what it takes to vindicate persistence realism (Section 2.2).

2.1 Persistence Error Theory and Persistence Realism

Persistence realism and persistence error theory involve two claims: a semantic claim and an ontological claim. The first is a claim about what our persistence sentences *mean*. It's a claim about the conditions under which those sentences are true. The second is a claim about the way our world is. Only when we put these together can we work out whether persistence realism or persistence error theory is vindicated.

To see this, notice that if we want to know whether 'there is a dog' is true or not, we need to know what 'there is a dog' means. We need to know which ways our world could be such that the claim is true and which ways such that it is false. When we specify what it would take to make that sentence true (or not) we make a *semantic claim*. Once we know the conditions under which that sentence is true or not, we can look to see what our world contains and see whether what it contains meets those conditions or not. If it does, then the sentence is true, if it does not, then it is not true. Claims about what our world contains are *ontological claims*. So, by combining a semantic claim and an ontological claim we can determine whether a sentence such as 'there is a dog' is true.

Persistence error theory involves the following claims.

> **Semantic claim:** Persistence sentences are true iff δ.

> **Ontological claim:** It is not the case that δ.

Persistence realism involves the following claims.[3]

> **Semantic claim:** Persistence sentences are true iff φ

> **Ontological claim:** It is the case that φ.

In order to understand and evaluate these claims, of course, we have to spell out the missing ingredient: the δ/φ. This is the task I take up next.

2.2 The Semantic Claim

Before I introduce several different views about how to spell out the semantic claim, I first want to introduce a central distinction between two views regarding the way in which actual objects are thought to persist. The next two sections will be spent fleshing out this distinction and making it more rigorous, and then putting it to use in framing answers to the semantic question. But for now, I just want to present the intuitive idea.

Imagine an ordinary object such as the statue Herbert. (Herbert is a statue of a chap, Herbert, and the statue's name is also Herbert; sometimes I will refer to

---

[3] Where it's an open question whether δ = φ. That is, it's an open question whether the persistence error theorist and persistence realist agree about what it would *take* for our concept of persistence to be satisfied, but disagree about whether or not it is (because they disagree about the ontological facts) or instead, agree about the ontological facts, but disagree about what it would *take* for our concept of persistence to be satisfied.

Herbert the statue as *it*, and sometimes as *he*, but I am always referring to the statue not the man the statue represents.)

Consider Herbert at a moment in time. At that time Herbert is *extended* in space. He takes up a region of space. He has a top and a bottom, a back and a front. Herbert is extended in space by having different parts at different locations. Herbert fills up one portion of space – one region – by having a head located at that region, and Herbert fills up another region by having a foot located at that region, and so on. Herbert is located at the region of space that contains all of his parts at a time.

Now let's consider Herbert across time. One possibility is that Herbert is extended through space in very much the same way that he is extended through time; a second possibility is that the way Herbert is extended through time is very different from the way he is extended through space.

According to the first kind of view, Herbert is a four-dimensional object spread out in space–time (where space–time is the aggregation of the three spatial dimensions and the fourth, temporal dimension, into a single thing) by having different parts located at different times. So only a *part* of Herbert is located at each time at which he exists. On that view, the statue-shaped object that exists at one time *is a different object* from the statue-shaped object that exists at any other time, in just the same way that Herbert's arm is a different object from his leg and his head. So, at any moment at which we look over at Herbert we are not seeing *all* of Herbert; we are just seeing one of the many parts of Herbert. Herbert *himself* is the collection of all of these parts; he is a four-dimensional object. This is the view that Herbert *perdures*.

By contrast, according to the second kind of view, when we see Herbert at any moment in time we see *all of* Herbert. Whereas Herbert is spread out in space by having different parts at different spatial regions, it is not the case that Herbert is extended through time by having different parts at different 'temporal' regions. Rather, Herbert exists at one time and then *the very same object*, Herbert, exists at the next time. What we see, when we look at Herbert at a moment in time, is not just one part of Herbert, but Herbert himself. So, on this view one and the same object is to be found at multiple times. Or, as we might put it, Herbert is *multiply located*. On this view Herbert is not a four-dimensional object that is spread out though time the way he is spread out through space: rather, Herbert is a three-dimensional object that is first located at one time, and then at another, and so on. This is the view that Herbert *endures*.[4]

---

[4] The terms endurance and perdurance are first mentioned by Johnston (1983) and become popularised by Lewis (1986).

I'll have much more to say about endurance and perdurance (and other views as well) as I articulate several different ways of spelling out the semantic claim. That's because these ways of spelling out the semantic claim appeal to the notions of endurance, perdurance, and others besides.

2.2.1 Endurance

Let's start by getting clearer on the idea of endurance. In what follows I will work with an eternalist picture of reality, on which past, present, and future objects (and events and properties) exist.[5] But this can be translated into claims about what did exist, does exist, and will exist. I think one can even make sense of my talk of four-dimensional regions by translating such talk into talk of a set or plurality of distinct three-dimensional regions where the members of that set/plurality do, did, or will exist. For simplicity though, I will simply talk *as though* eternalism is true. Non-eternalists can (I hope) still make good sense of all that follows (and can translate it into a non-eternalist framework).

So, what do we mean by the claim that 'all of' an object exists at multiple times? To get some traction on this idea I will suppose that we can talk of the relations – *locative relations* – that obtain between an object and the region at which it exists.[6] This will make it much easier to see the difference between enduring and perduring objects.

In what follows I follow Gilmore (2007) in taking *exact location* to be primitive. We can give an informal gloss on exact location by saying that an object O is exactly located at region R when R shares the same size and shape as O and stands in the same spatio-temporal relations to other objects as O does. Then an object endures just in case that object has multiple exact locations over time.

Imagine we are looking down on a block of space–time that includes all the objects (and events) that exist (i.e., past, present, and future ones). Let's consider Herbert again. Suppose, for simplicity, that Herbert begins to exist at t_2 and remains in existence until t_7. At each time at which Herbert exists, he is statue-shaped and he fills up a statue-shaped region of space. Each of those regions is three-dimensional. That's because at each time he exists, Herbert has length, breadth, and width, and so he fills up a three-dimensional statue-shaped region of space. That means that when we look 'down' on space–time (from outside of it – this is of course only a useful heuristic device) we see that Herbert 'fills up' a *four*-dimensional region of space–time. He fills up a statue-shaped

---

[5] For defenses of eternalism (in its B-theoretic guise) see Le Poidevin (1991); Price (1996); Mellor (1998); Savitt (2002); Maudlin (2007); Farr (2012, 2020); Ismael (2012, 2017); Oaklander (2012); Bardon (2013); Deng; (2013a, 2013b, 2019); Leininger (2018, 2021).

[6] For discussion of location and location relations, see Parsons (2007, 2008) and Eagle (2010a, 2010b).

three-dimensional region at t_2, and another one at t_3, and another one at t_4, and so on. In all, Herbert fills the four-dimensional region that is composed of each of these statue-shaped three-dimensional regions.[7] With this in mind, we can now make better sense of the idea that enduring objects are multiply located over time.

Following Eagle (2010a) let's say that an object *fills* a region, R, just in case none of R is free from the object: that is, there is no sub-region of R at which (some of) the object cannot be found. Consider the glass in front of me. The glass is *filled* with water because none of the glass is free of water. There's water everywhere in the glass. If we think of the glass as standing in for a region, then the region in question is filled with water.

Further, let's say that an object is *contained* in a region, R, just in case none of that object is located outside of R. So, for instance, the room I am sitting in contains a couch. The couch is contained in the room since none of it is located outside of the room. If we move the couch so that it is partly in the hallway and partly in the living room, then it will no longer be contained in the living room.

While the couch is *contained* in the living room it does not *fill* that room, since there is (thankfully) plenty of the living room that is free of the couch (all those places where the couch is not located).

Now let us say that when an object is both *contained* in, and *fills*, some region, it is *fully located* in that region.

Full location: O is fully located at a region, R, iff O both fills and is contained in R.

So, suppose my couch only exists for a single moment of time, t. Consider the couch-shaped region at t. That region is one at which the couch is fully located. That's because the couch *fills* that region (nowhere in the region is free of the couch) and is contained in the region (none of the couch is outside of that region).

This notion of full location is going to be important. That's because any object that in some sense or other exists at multiple times will be one that is fully located at a four-dimensional region. My instantaneous couch is fully located at a *three*-dimensional couch-shaped region, but that's because it is instantaneous.

Since there are different ways in which an object can be fully located at a four-dimensional region, it follows that there can be different accounts of what it takes for persistence sentences to be true.

---

[7] At this point it is worth briefly saying something about how I am conceiving of four-dimensional regions. When we imagine regions, we typically imagine them as continuous: that is, as having no gaps between their various sub-regions. We imagine one uninterrupted region. As I will use the term, regions need not be continuous. So the following is a four-dimensional region: the region that is composed of a three-dimensional region at t_2, a three-dimensional region at t_4, and a three-dimensional region at t_6. That region is spatio-temporally disconnected but is four-dimensional nonetheless.

Let's return to Herbert. Herbert is fully located in a four-dimensional region. Let's call that region H (for Herbert). How does Herbert fill H? Following Eagle, let's introduce the idea of an M-region. An M-region is a maximally temporally unextended (i.e., three-dimensional) sub-region of a full location of an object. Each M-region corresponds to what we can think of as the region occupied by an object *at a moment of time*. So, earlier we said that Herbert is located at a three-dimensional statue-shaped region at t_2 and another at t_3. Each of these three-dimensional regions are M-regions.

If Herbert endures then he is exactly located at each M-region. Moreover, Herbert is fully located at the four-dimensional region H *by being exactly located* at each M-region. We can then define endurance as follows:

> **Endure**: An object, O, endures iff O is fully located at a four-dimensional region, R, and O is exactly located at each M-region in R.

Objects that endure are first exactly located at one (three-dimensional) region, and then at another, and then another. They are fully located at four-dimensional regions by being exactly located at a series of three-dimensional regions. So, if Herbert endures, then first we find Herbert at one time (one M-region) and in doing so we find, as it were, all of Herbert. Then we find Herbert at another time, and, again, in doing so we find all of Herbert. Herbert exists through time by being multiply located through time: by first being exactly located at one time, and then at the next, and then at the next. Another way to put this is that when we find Herbert at one time, and then at another, we are finding one and the same statue: Herbert. The statue-shaped object that we find at one time is *numerically identical* with the statue-shaped object we find at another time. That is, the statue-shaped object that is exactly located at one M-region is numerically identical to the statue-shaped object that is exactly located at another M-region. That is because there is really just one object, Herbert, and we find that object – all of that object – located at each of those M-regions.

Let us say that one is an *endurantist* if one thinks that actual objects endure.[8] If we consider our second question, 'how do actual objects persist?', the answer 'they endure' is a very popular answer among philosophers.

According to endurantists, persistence sentences are made true by there being enduring objects (of the right sort). So, consider 'Annie was small and fluffy'. According to endurantists this sentence is made true by the fact that Annie has multiple exact locations and one of those locations is earlier than the time at

---

[8] Defences of endurantism (not all of them by endurantists) can be found in Thomson (1983, 1998); Lowe (1987); van Inwagen (1990b); Merricks (1994, 1999a); Hinchliff (1996); Rea (1998); Klein (1999); Miller (2004, 2008); Oderberg (2004); Brower (2010); Daniels (2013); Magidor (2016); Pezet (2019).

which we are assessing the sentence, and Annie, at that location, is small and fluffy.

Crucially, if persistence sentences that mention 'O' are true in virtue of there being some object, O, that endures then: (a) 'O' picks out a single enduring object, and (b) O is exactly located at more than one M-region, and (c) the object, O, that is exactly located at one M-region is numerically identical to the object, O, that is exactly located at another M-region. This is the sense in which enduring objects are multiply located and the sense in which enduring objects are numerically identical over time.

Rather than thinking of endurantism as just a view about the way ordinary objects persist, we can imagine someone offering something like this view as an answer to our question: under what conditions are persistence sentences true? We can call the view that results from this *semantic endurantism*.[9] Then the semantic endurantist will say something like the following:

> **Semantic endurantism:** Persistence sentences are true iff (relevant)[10] objects endure.

According to semantic endurantism, what it takes for persistence sentences to be true is for there to be the (right) enduring objects.

Why might one endorse semantic endurantism? Well, it is often thought that it seems to each of us, in experience, as though objects persist by being numerically identical over time and thus that we represent the world as containing enduring objects.[11] Consider: 'Last week I picked lemons, and tomorrow I will cook with them.' It is natural to think (or so the thought goes) that there is a single object, me, all of whom existed yesterday, exists today, and will exist

---

[9] Many of the argument for endurantism are also arguments for semantic endurantism. For instance, arguments that appeal to the idea that absent endurance, objects don't really change, are probably best interpreted as reasons to endorse semantic endurantism (see, for instance, Klein (1999); Hinchliff (1996); and Oderberg (2004) – and for arguments to the contrary see Hales and Johnson (2003)). That's because they aim to show not simply that it is in fact the presence of enduring things that makes true many of our ordinary persistence sentences, but rather, that in the absence of enduring things those sentences would all be false (since persistence sentences are, very often, about changing persisting things). By contrast, sometimes arguments for endurantism appear to be ones that do not provide us with reasons to endorse semantic endurantism. For instance, the idea that endurantism is not consistent with special relativity (or at least, is a poor fit with the view) have been offered by Balashov (2000a, 2000b, 2000c) and Hales and Johnson (2003) (for arguments to the contrary see Miller 2004). But at most, these arguments would seem to suggest that actual objects do not endure, and hence that what makes true, ordinary persistence sentences is not enduring things. That leaves open that semantic endurantism might be true, and hence that persistence error theory might be vindicated. So, such arguments are not really arguments against semantic endurantism.

[10] It is not enough that there are enduring objects; they have to be the relevant ones to make true the sentences in question.

[11] See, for instance, Velleman (2006) and Prosser (2012).

tomorrow, such that the me of yesterday, the me of today, and the me of tomorrow, are all *the very same thing: me*.[12] So, it seems natural to say that if there are enduring objects, then our persistence sentences are true. If that is right, then the presence of (relevant) enduring objects is sufficient to make true the persistence sentences that we take to be true, or, as I will sometimes put it, endurance is *sufficient* for persistence.

One might also think that the presence of (relevant) enduring objects is *necessary* to make true the various persistence sentences that we take to be true, or, as I will sometimes put it, that endurance is *necessary* for persistence. We noted earlier that it seems roughly right to think that an object persists just in case it exists at multiple times. The question then arises, what is it to exist at multiple times? Well, one might think, *what it is* to exist at multiple times is to endure. What we *mean* when we say that Herbert exists at multiple times is precisely that we find Herbert at one time, and then we find Herbert himself at another time. What we do not mean, for instance, is that we find a part of Herbert at one time, and some other, distinct part of Herbert at some other time. So, we might think, persistence sentences can only be true if objects endure.

Here's a second reason to think this might be so. It seems very plausible that ordinary persistence sentences – the various sentences that you and I utter and think and take to be true – can only be true if persisting objects genuinely *change*. Indeed, persistence and change seem to be inextricably connected. Objects can surely only change if they persist, since to change requires that something exists at multiple times. Many apparently true persistence sentences report on such changes (just go back and look at the description that began this Element). But, as we will explore further in Section 5, you might think that change requires endurance. That is because you might think that what it takes for, say, Herbert to change, is for Herbert himself to exist at different times and for Herbert to be different at those different times. Herbert does not count as *changing*, you might think, if he simply has some parts that are one way and other parts that are some other way. After all, we don't think that Herbert *changes* just because at a particular time, his feet are different from his head! Yet this is just how Herbert would 'change' over time if Herbert existed across time by having different parts at different times.[13] So, you might think,

---

[12] As we will see in Section 2.2.3, we need to be a bit careful here since on views of persistence on which persisting objects are not numerically identical across time in this sense (by being composed of distinct objects at times) there is still some sense in which they are numerically identical across time: namely, the sense in which they are extended across time and they (like everything else) are identical to themselves.

[13] See Hinchliff (1996); Klein (1999); and Oderberg (2004).

persistence sentences cannot be true unless objects endure. These considerations might push us to accept semantic endurantism.

Semantic endurantism is what I will call a *demanding* view. It makes it relatively easy to see how persistence error theory could turn out to be true. For it entails that if objects do not endure, then persistence error theory is true. As such, it's a view on which the semantics for ordinary persistence sentences are such that the world might seem to us just as it does, and yet persistence error theory is true. So the view is demanding in that it demands (if persistence sentences are to be true) that the world has a certain underlying metaphysical nature (endurance) which might for all we know be one that is missing in our world. That is, things might seem to us as they do, and yet the world lacks this metaphysical nature and hence none of our persistence sentences are true.

Before I move on to articulate our next view about the conditions under which persistence sentences are true, first I want to take a short detour. I've just introduced the idea that our world might seem the way that it does to us, and yet none of our persistence sentences are true. But what does it mean to talk about how our world *seems* to us? Since this is going to be important in what follows, it's worth stopping and considering this issue.

2.2.2 How Do Things Seem to Us?

What do I mean by the idea that the world *seems to us to be some way?* Consider the experience of seeing a red ball. The 'what it's like' to see the ball is known as the *phenomenal character* of the experience. When I see a red ball, or feel a sharp pain, I have experiences that have phenomenal character. What it's like to see a red ball is very different from what it's like to feel a sharp pain. So, the phenomenal character of these two experiences is different. Perceptual experiences, like seeing a red ball, usually have both a phenomenal character and a *representational content*. The representational content of the experience is what it is that the experience represents. It is what the experience is *about*. If I am seeing a red ball, then my perceptual experience represents a red ball. So, when I see a red ball my experience represents that there is a red ball (the representational content of the experience) and there is something that it is like to have the experience of seeing the red ball (the phenomenal character of the experience). It is common to think that what it's like to have that experience (its phenomenal character) is determined by the representational content of the experience: by the fact that the experience represents a red ball rather than, say, a purple sphere.

The *phenomenal content* of a perceptual experience is the aspect of the representational content of that experience that determines its phenomenal character. To get a handle on what I mean here, suppose I keep a box of rubber balls in the cupboard. The balls come in five different colours. Weirdly, I give each ball a name. One day I look down at the carpet and see a bright red rubber ball. The ball is in fact Jeremy. So it is part of the representational content of my perceptual experience that the experience represents Jeremy. But if instead I had been looking at Suzy (another bright red rubber ball) things would have looked the same. The two experiences have the same phenomenal character. That aspect of their representational content that determines this character is their phenomenal content. The phenomenal content is indistinguishable in these two cases: it's (roughly) *its seeming that there is a bright red rubber ball on the floor.*

When I talk about the world seeming to us to be some way, it is the phenomenal contents of our experiences that I have in mind. Among the various ways things seem to us, there is a way (or ways) that will be of particular importance in what follows. Consider a perfectly ordinary experience in which you are sitting on a couch. You feel the couch under you and you see it around you. It seems to you (I say), as you sit there, as though the couch at one time is very *similar* to the couch at the previous and at the next times. It seems as though the couch at one time is in a very similar (or the same) location, and has very similar, or the same, properties as the couch at temporally adjacent times. If you sit there long enough perhaps the couch changes a little; perhaps you drop crumbs on it, and, if you sit there a really long time, perhaps it fades, or loses some of its support. But whatever changes it goes through, it will seem similar throughout any relatively short period of time.

I think it also seems to you as though you can *intervene* on the couch in various ways. If you spill liquid on it now, it gets wet, and it remains wet at some later times (but not at earlier ones). If you move one end of the couch now, then it will be moved at later, but not earlier, times (until you move it back). If you want the couch to be a different colour in a month's time, you can bring that about by having it recovered, or spray-painted, or whatever else, now.

In all, we might say that you have a series of *couch-at-times* experiences – experiences that seem to be experiences of a couch, at a time – and that it is part of the phenomenal content of these experiences that the couch at one time is very *similar* to the couch at adjacent times (*similarity*); that the couch at one time is in a spatially similar location to the couch at adjacent times (*spatial contiguity*) (the couch might move, but it doesn't suddenly disappear from one location and appear miles away from one moment to the next; if it's in your lounge at t_1, then it is also in your lounge at t_2); that you do not experience the couch as existing at one time, and then not at the next, and then existing again after that (*temporal continuity*); that it seems to you as though you can causally intervene on the nature of the couch at later times, by intervening on it at earlier times (*intervention*); and, more broadly, that it seems to you as though the way the couch is, at later times, is a function of how the couch is, at earlier times (*dependence*).

These experiences are not peculiar to couches! These are the sorts of experiences that we have all the time, and which seem to be inextricably connected with there being persisting things. I will call experiences like this *P-experiences* (P for persistence). P-experiences are the experiences we have which lead us to say that there are persisting things. They are the experiences we have which lead us to say things like 'Annie was much smaller as a puppy' and 'the couch is really dirty today compared to yesterday, did someone eat a bone on it?' and so on. If we didn't have P-experiences, then we would experience the world as being populated by a series of disconnected, unrelated, things. It would not seem to us as though we can change the orientation of the couch by moving it. It would not seem to us as though the reason the couch is dirty, now, is because Annie ate a bone on it, earlier, or that the reason it is faded, now, is because of the impact of the sun over many years. It would not seem to us as though Annie, now, is similar to Annie a moment ago; nor that her location, now, is similar to her location a moment ago. If things did not seem like this, they would seem radically different to the ways they do seem. Indeed, I am inclined to say that it would no longer seem to us as though objects persist at all.

I am going to use the phrase *gen-identity* to refer to the relation, or set of relations (probably the latter), that 'stand behind' or 'ground' our having P-experiences. In this regard, I am using the term rather differently from how it is sometimes used. Lewin (1922) introduced the term gen-identity to pick out the relationship that exists between an object at one time, and an object at another time, such that the ways the later object is depends on the ways the earlier objects are, and, indeed, perhaps the very existence of the later object depends on the existence of the earlier objects. As introduced by Lewin, gen-identity relations are relations that obtain between *distinct* momentary objects. Moreover, they are often characterised in terms of the obtaining of certain dependence relations between an object at one time, and an object at another time.

My use of the term will depart from this in several ways. As I use the term, it simply picks out *whichever* relations it is, in our world, that grounds its being the case that we have P-experiences. First, unlike Lewin, I am not assuming that gen-identity relations can only obtain between distinct momentary objects. Indeed, I do not assume that gen-identity relations must obtain between an *object* at one time, and an *object* at some other time. Rather, it might be that gen-identity relations obtain between the properties of an object at one time, and the properties of an object at another time. So, on this way of understanding gen-identity, it is compatible with identity over time. Consider some enduring object, O. I will often talk loosely about O at one time being gen-identity related to O at some other time: this will be true if there are relations that obtain between O's properties at one time and O's properties at another time; there being these relations is what grounds our having the P-experiences we do. For instance, perhaps O's having the properties it does, at later times, is the causal product of O having the properties it does, at earlier times.

Further, I make no assumptions about what relations it is that ground our P-experiences. It could be, for instance, that in our world in addition to there being similarity relations, and relations of spatial and temporal contiguity and continuity, there are also substantial causal relations that obtain between momentary objects, or between the properties of an object at one time and an object at another time, and that it is these, jointly, that constitute gen-identity. Perhaps, for instance, causal relations are the product of things 'banging into' one another (metaphorically speaking) and leaving causal marks or traces. Such views of causation are known as *process* theories of causation.[14] These are fairly metaphysically 'weighty' theories, on which causation involves physical processes in our world and is something more than there merely being certain true counterfactuals of the form, if c had not happened then e would not have happened. Equally, perhaps gen-identity relations are, partly, constituted by there being special sui generis asymmetric dependence relations, such that momentary objects at later times *existentially depend* on earlier momentary objects.[15] On this view, the world contains what we might think of as 'levers' that connect up objects at different times. These levers are the dependence relations and it is because they obtain that 'pushing on' one object by, say, intervening on it certain ways, 'pushes on' the other object: it does this via the lever between them. If there exist these sorts of relations, then gen-identity relations will, in part, consist in there being these relations.

Equally though, it might be that our world does not contain special dependence relations and that causation is not an oomphy matter of one thing leaving a causal mark on another. Perhaps, for instance, causation is nothing more than counterfactual dependence, so that, very roughly, x causes y when, had x not happened then y would not have happened. Perhaps all there really is, which grounds there being P-experiences, is our world having a certain kind of Humean pattern to it. For instance, perhaps all that grounds our having P-experiences is that there are certain patterns of similarity, continuity, and contiguity over time, such that given those patterns we can predict what will

---

[14] See, for instance, Salmon (1994) and Dowe (2009).
[15] For instance, see Correia (2005) and Lowe (1994, 2013)

happen at later times, on the basis of how things are at earlier times, and on the basis of what we do at earlier times. We can, for instance, predict that if we put the salt in the warm water it will dissolve, for in our world there exists a robust pattern of salt dissolving in warm water. Because there are these patterns, we have experiences in which it seems to us that we can bring it about that things are a certain way later by making it the case that they are a certain way now.

Crucially, gen-identity relations, as I am conceiving of them, are just whatever relations it is, in our world, that we are tracking when we have P-experiences. This is going to be important. For, as I have set things up, we can be confident that there are gen-identity relations. How so? Well, clearly we cannot be confident that there are sui generis dependence relations, or that there are robust causal relations of the kind posited by process theorists. Our world could seem the same to us, in experience, as it does – it could have the same phenomenal contents – and yet it could turn out that our world doesn't contain any sui generis dependence relations, or any robust causal relations.

So, if gen-identity relations were, or were partly, constated by such relations, then we would have no way to be sure that there are such relations. Notably, though, this is not the view I have in mind. The view I have in mind says that gen-identity relations are the relations that ground, or explain, or are tracked by our having P-experiences. Hence, it is consistent with there being such relations that our world merely contains certain robust patterns and that it is the existence of these patterns that our P-experiences track. If that turns out to be so, then it will still turn out that there are gen-identity relations.

So, there are two important things to take away from our discussion here. First, given that we have P-experiences, we can be confident that there are gen-identity relations. What we cannot be confident of, is just what relations those are. Second, the world could seem to us just as it does, and *yet contain no enduring objects*. That's because we could have the very same P-experiences and yet our world might contain, say, perduring objects instead of enduring ones. This is why I say that semantic endurantism entails that the world could seem to us just as it does, and persistence error theory turn out to be true. In turn, that's why I say the view is relatively demanding.

We can now appeal to the idea of perdurance to generate a different way of spelling out the semantic claim.

2.2.3 Perdurance

The view that objects perdure is the view that they are extended through time in the same way they are extended through space: by having distinct (short-lived) parts located at different times.

To get a better handle on this view imagine, once again, that we are looking down on Herbert in space–time. Herbert, recall, is fully located at four-dimensional region H. If Herbert perdures, then Herbert is fully located at H in virtue of being *exactly* located at H.

To see this, consider each M-region of H. Remember that an M-region is just a three-dimensional region of space at which an object is located at a particular time. If Herbert perdures, then at each M-region there is, exactly located, a numerically distinct momentary object. These momentary objects are each part of Herbert: they are each its *temporal parts*. Then Herbert is exactly located at H in virtue of being composed of all (and only) these parts. Therefore, just as when we look at Herbert at a particular time and notice that it is extended through space by having *spatial* parts (the various parts of the statue), so too on this view Herbert is extended through time by having various *temporal* parts.[16]

So, where the endurantist thinks that at each M-region it's the whole of Herbert that exists and that Herbert is multiply located across H, the perdurantist thinks that at each M-region it's a proper part of Herbert that exists and Herbert is the whole four-dimensional object made up of those parts, which is exactly located at H. Thus, on this view Herbert is not multiply located. Herbert has a single location, and that location is a four-dimensional one.

We can define perdurance as follows:

> **Perdure**: An object, O, perdures iff O is exactly located at a four-dimensional region, R, and for each M-region of R, there is a temporal part of O that is exactly located at that M-region.

Then let us call someone a *perdurantist* if they hold that actual objects persist by perduring.[17] According to perdurantists, the answer to our second question, 'how do objects persist?', is 'they perdure'. According to perdurantists, persistence sentences are made true by the ways that four-dimensional objects are, at times. That is, they are made true by the ways the temporal parts of those four-dimensional objects are. So 'Annie was small and fluffy' is made true by the fact that Annie is a four-dimensional object that is composed of temporal parts some

---

[16] This way of framing things makes it sound as though there is a direction of dependence that runs from the temporal parts to the whole: that is, that the whole is the way it is because of the way the parts are; the whole is fully located where it is because of where each of its parts is. Many versions of perdurantism take this to be so since it is most natural to suppose that wholes depend on their parts rather than the other way around. Strictly speaking though, one could think that wholes are prior to their parts and still endorse the view that objects perdure. One would simply think that it is four-dimensional wholes that are fundamental, and their parts depend on those wholes. For discussion of this issue, see Wasserman (2016).

[17] Perdurantists, or those who have defended perdurantism in various ways, include Quine (1950); Lewis (1976, 1986); Armstrong (1980); Heller (1984, 1990); Balashov (2000a, 2000b, 2000c); Hudson (2001); Sider (2001); Hales and Johnson (2003); Miller (2009); and Wasserman (2016).

of which are in the past (relative to the time at which we are evaluating the sentence in question) and some of those past temporal parts are small and fluffy. Crucially, if persistence sentences that mention 'O' are true in virtue of there being some object, O, that perdures then: (a) 'O' picks out a single perduring object; (b) O is exactly located at a single four-dimensional region; and (c) the object, O*, that is exactly located at one M-region is numerically distinct from any other object, O**, that is exactly located at another M-region.

Importantly, sometimes the temporal parts of perduring objects are causally connected in a way that most other momentary objects are not. If ordinary objects perdure, then their temporal parts are connected in this sort of way.

Consider Herbert. If Herbert perdures, then there is a momentary object located just at t_1, another located just at t_2, and another located just at t_3. There are three distinct objects. Each of them looks like a statue. Each is a temporal part of Herbert.

Suppose, as described earlier, I paint the leg of one of those momentary objects purple. What do I expect to see? I expect to see that the leg of each of the temporally later momentary statue-like objects is also purple (until I engage in some cleaning). The relationship between the momentary objects that are temporal parts of ordinary objects, then, is quite different from the relationship between other distinct objects. The way the momentary statue-shaped object is at t_3 depends on how the momentary statue-shaped object is at t_2. There is a counterfactual dependence that obtains between the statue-shaped object at one time and the statue-shaped object at another time. That is, had the earlier statue-shaped objects been different from how they are, then the later statue-shaped objects would also be different from how they are; the later objects counterfactually depend on the earlier ones. Indeed, it may often be not just that the *way* later momentary objects are is a matter of how earlier momentary objects are, but that the very existence of these later objects depends on the existence of the earlier ones. If, for instance, I destroy an earlier statue-shaped object on my mantelpiece, then there will be no later statue-shaped objects.

We can now appeal to the idea of perdurance to generate a different way of spelling out the semantic claim. Call someone a *semantic perdurantist* if they hold that persistence sentences are true iff there exist (relevant) perduring objects.[18]

> **Semantic perdurantism:** Persistence sentences are true iff (relevant) objects perdure.

---

[18] Again, many arguments for perdurantism are also arguments for semantic perdurantism, though some are not.

Why might one endorse semantic perdurantism? Well, one might think it plausible that perdurance is sufficient for persistence. If there are (relevant) four-dimensional regions at which some object is fully located then (the thought goes) that is enough for our persistence sentences to be true. This captures the sense in which you might think that all that is required for persistence is that objects exist at multiple times. Clearly objects that are fully located at a four-dimension region *do* exist at multiple times, regardless of how it is that they fill and are contained in that region. So if one has this view one will conclude that this is sufficient to render true our ordinary persistence sentences.

One might also think that perdurance is necessary for persistence. As already noted, one might think that persistence sentences can be true only if objects genuinely change. And, as I will discuss in Section 5, one might think that it is only by having different parts at different times that objects *can* change. So, unless objects perdure, one might think, they cannot change, and hence our ordinary persistence sentences cannot be true. That is why perdurance is necessary for persistence.

Semantic perdurantism, like semantic endurantism, is a demanding view in that it's a view on which the world might seem to us to be the way it does, and yet persistence error theory is true. This will be the case if, for instance, actual objects endure rather than perdure.

2.2.3.1 Is Endurance Different from Perdurance?

At this point you might perhaps be wondering if endurance *really* is different from perdurance, or if these two accounts are two different ways of describing the same underlying reality or metaphysical facts. The idea captured by this thought is that the two views are *metaphysically equivalent*[19] – that endurantists and perdurantists are using two different languages, or sets of terminology, to describe the same facts. This idea has been defended by several authors (an earlier incarnation of myself included).[20] The issues here are complex. Miller (2005a) for instance, offers us a translation manual for moving between the sentences that the perdurantist takes to be true, and those the endurantist takes to be true, and tries to show that not only can we translate endurantist talk into perdurantist talk and vice versa, but that the two views have the same explanatory power, and hence that we should conclude that they are not really distinct at all.

In the remainder of this Element, though, I will assume that these two views are distinct. In part this is because this is the view of most of those

---

[19] For more on metaphysical equivalence, see Miller (2005c, 2017).
[20] See McCall and Lowe (2002); Miller (2005a); and Wahlberg (2014).

working in the area, and it would take us far afield to try to evaluate the arguments here. Moreover, I think that once we conceive of these views in terms of the different relations that objects bear to the regions of space–time at which they are located, it is prima facie plausible that the views are distinct. Here is why.

Endurantists say that persisting objects are exactly located at multiple three-dimensional regions and are not exactly located at any four-dimensional region. Perdurantists say that persisting objects are exactly located at a single four-dimensional region and are not exactly located at multiple three-dimensional regions. So endurantists and perdurantists certainly *seem* to disagree. They disagree about how objects are related to the regions of space–time at which they exist.

The only way it could turn out that endurantists and perdurantists are not really disagreeing is if they disagree about the meanings of at least one locational term that we've used to define the ways in which enduring and perduring objects are related to the regions of space–time at which they exist.

We've now defined most of the various locational terms at issue (such as fill and containment and full location) earlier in this Element. And endurantists and perdurantists can and do sign up to these definitions. So, we have some reason to think that they mean the same thing by these expressions.

Given this, the most likely hypothesis is that they disagree about what 'exact location' means. Since that's a primitive notion, it lacks a definition. So perhaps when endurantists say that persisting objects have three-dimensional exact locations, and perdurantists say that they have a single four-dimensional exact location, they are really saying the same thing because they mean something different by 'exact location'.

Maybe so. An exact location is supposed to be the place where we find, as it were, 'all' of the object: the place that is the same size, shape, and so on, as the object itself. This seems like an intuitive notion that endurantists and perdurantists can share, and it's not obvious what two distinct notions could be at play here such that one party is employing one notion, and the other party the other notion. None of this is to say that we should be certain that the views are distinct or that, ultimately, we will not come to the view that they are not distinct. But for now, it makes sense to treat them as though they are distinct.

2.2.4 Transdurance

This brings us to our third way of spelling out the semantic claim. This account appeals to the idea of transdurance rather than either endurance or perdurance.

So, what is transdurance? Consider, again, Herbert. Remember, Herbert is fully located at four-dimensional region H. Herbert transdures if he is exactly located at H (as perdurantists suppose) but is not exactly located at H by being composed of any momentary objects that are each exactly located at each M-region of H. Rather, there are *no* objects exactly located at each M-region of H which are parts of Herbert. So, while Herbert is four-dimensional (since it's exactly located at H) it lacks any temporal parts: it is like a big extended simple (at least along the temporal dimension; it might still have spatial parts at a particular time).

Transdurantism is a little like endurantism and a little like perdurantism. It is like perdurantism in that it denies that persisting objects are multiply located over time. Transduring objects have a single exact location, which is four-dimensional. In this, transduring objects are like perduring objects. But it is like endurantism in that it holds that persisting objects are not made up of lots of momentary objects. Indeed, it can be that objects transdure even if there are no momentary objects. We can define transdurance as follows:

> **Transdure**: An object, O, transdures iff O is exactly located at a four-dimensional region, R, and there is no object, O*, that is exactly located at any M-region of O which is a part of O.[21]

Call someone a *transdurantist* if they hold that actual objects transdure. The transdurantist will say that persistence sentences are made true by transduring objects. The transdurantist will say that 'Annie was small and fluffy' is made true by Annie being a transduring object, which is, at some time in the past (i.e., earlier than the time at which we are evaluating the sentence) small and fluffy. Crucially, if persistence sentences that mention 'O' are true in virtue of there being something, O, that transdures then: (a) 'O' picks out a single transduring object and (b) O is exactly located at a single four-dimensional region.

We can now use the idea of transdurance to develop a third view about how to spell out the semantic claim. The resulting view is *semantic transdurantism*.[22]

---

[21] A view of this kind was probably first introduced by Parsons (2000). It was considered under the name of terdurantism by Miller (2009) and then defended under the name of transdurantism by Daniels (2013, 2014(b), 2019).

[22] Many of the arguments for endurantism are also arguments for semantic endurantism. For instance, arguments that appeal to the idea that absent endurance, objects don't really change, are surely best interpreted as reasons to endorse semantic endurantism (see, for example, Hinchliff (1996); Klein (1999); and Oderberg (2004)). Other arguments, however, are best interpreted as arguments to the conclusion that objects do not in fact endure (see, for example, Hales and Johnson (2003)). By contrast, sometimes arguments for endurantism appear to be ones that do not provide us with reason to endorse semantic endurantism. For instance, the idea that endurantism is not consistent with special relativity (or at least, is a poor fit with the view) has

Semantic transdurantism: Persistence sentences are true iff (relevant) objects transdure.

Like the other two views we have already encountered, semantic transdurantism is a demanding view. It entails that the world might seem just as it does to us, and yet it turns out that persistence error theory is true. That will be so if actual objects perdure or endure rather than transdure.

2.2.5 Exdurantism

Perdurantism is the view that objects persist by being composed of momentary objects and that it is the presence of these perduring objects that makes our ordinary persistence sentences true.

Suppose one agrees with the perdurantist that what exists at each time is a momentary object, but one holds that persisting objects are not *composed* of those objects. One might think this because one thinks that there is nothing that is composed of those momentary objects, or because one thinks that even if there is such an object, that object is not what makes persistence sentences true. According to *exdurantists* or *stage-theorists*, it is the presence of these momentary objects, and not the presence of any four-dimensional object, which makes ordinary persistence sentences true.[23]

According to exdurantists, ordinary expressions like 'the ball', 'Annie', and 'the statue' pick out momentary objects. So they don't pick out objects that are extended in time or which exist at multiple times. How, then, could any persistence sentence be true? On this view persistence sentences are made true by the existence of *temporal counterparts*, where temporal counterparts are themselves momentary objects.

Consider some set of momentary objects: the objects that according to the perdurantist, compose Annie, the labradoodle. According to the exdurantist, when we talk about Annie we are in fact talking about just *one* of these momentary objects (the one that exists now). But claims about what Annie did do, or will do, are made true by what *other* momentary objects in that set do. These other momentary objects are Annie's temporal counterparts.

Temporal counterparts are like modal counterparts, except they are (momentary) objects that exist at other times, not in other worlds.[24] So, just as (modal)

---

been offered by Balashov (2000a, 2000b, 2000c) and Hales and Johnson (2003). This would seem to be a reason to think that as a matter of fact objects do not endure (for arguments to the contrary, see Miller (2004)) but would appear to give us no reason either in favour of, or against, semantic endurantism.

[23] Defenders of such views include Sider (1996, 2000); Hawley (2001); Rychter (2012); and Parsons (2015).

[24] See Lewis (1986).

counterpart theorists hold that it is the existence of distinct objects in other possible worlds – namely, our modal counterparts – which make true various modal claims about how things could have been for each of us, so too exdurantists hold that it is the presence of temporal counterparts – distinct objects at other times – that make true various diachronic claims about how things were, or will be, for each of us.

According to modal counterpart theory what makes it true that you could have been wealthy (say) is that you have a counterpart that is wealthy.[25] That counterpart is not you: it's numerally distinct from you. But the fact that your counterpart is wealthy is what makes it true that you could have been wealthy. So, the property of *being possibly wealthy* is yours – it is attributed to you – but your having that property consists in you bearing a relationship to an object that is not you, and is wealthy.

Likewise, 'Annie was small and fluffy' is true just in case Annie, the momentary object picked out by 'Annie' has a past temporal counterpart that is small and fluffy. It is Annie who has the property of having once been small and fluffy, but she has it in virtue of bearing a relation to a distinct object, a temporal counterpart, that is small and fluffy.

Standard exdurantists agree with perdurantists when it comes to ontology. They agree with perdurantists that there are four-dimensional objects composed of momentary temporal parts. But while the perdurantist thinks that ordinary expressions like 'the lemon' and 'Annie' and 'the statue' pick out four-dimensional objects, the standard exdurantist thinks that these expressions pick out momentary temporal parts of those objects. While the perdurantist thinks that 'Annie was small and fluffy' is made true by the fact that Annie, the four-dimensional object, has a past temporal part that is small is fluffy, the standard exdurantist thinks that 'Annie was small and fluffy' is made true by the fact that Annie is a momentary object that has a past temporal counterpart that is small and fluffy.

By contrast, what we might call *non-standard exdurantism* holds that there are no four-dimensional objects, and hence disagrees with the perdurantist about ontology. Non-standard exdurantists hold that there exist just the various momentary objects connected by various relations. Standard and non-standard exdurantists agree, though, about what makes ordinary persistence claims true: namely, that it is the presence of temporal counterparts.

We can now use this picture of exdurantism to provide yet another way of spelling out the semantic claim: *semantic exdurantism*.

---

[25] See Lewis (1986) for a canonical defence of this view.

Semantic exdurantism: Persistence sentences are true iff (relevant) objects exdure (i.e., iff objects are three-dimensional and have temporal counterparts).

Again, semantic exdurantism is demanding in that it leaves open that, for all we know, persistence error theory is true. That will be so if there are no exduring objects because, say, objects endure or transdure.

These four ways of spelling out the semantic claim each appeal to one of the four major views – endurance, perdurance, transdurance, and exdurance – about the way actual objects persist. In what follows I consider two further ways of spelling out the semantic claim that are less well discussed.

2.2.6 Successionism

Consider, for a moment, non-standard exdurantism. That view rejects the existence of four-dimensional objects, maintaining that there only exist pluralities of distinct momentary objects. It then offers a new way of understanding in virtue of what persistence sentences are true. According to that view, ordinary expressions pick out momentary objects. What is surprising about this view is that sentences that *appear* to be about things that exist at more than one time are made true even though in fact our ordinary expressions pick out momentary objects, and hence objects that *do not* exist at more than one time.

Successionism is also a surprising view, but the surprise is located somewhere different.

Successionists agree with non-standard exdurantists that there only exist pluralities of momentary objects. And they agree that it is the existence of these pluralities that makes our ordinary persistence sentences true. But rather than saying that ordinary expressions pick out momentary objects, and that it is the presence of temporal counterparts that makes these ordinary sentences true, the successionist says that what appear, *grammatically*, to be singular referring terms, such as 'the lemon' and 'Annie' and 'Herbert' are not really singular referring terms at all. They refer to pluralities of objects: to pluralities of appropriately connected momentary objects. 'Annie', for instance, refers to the plurality of momentary labradoodle-y objects that are connected by a relation of gen-identity. So, in ordinary English, when we talk about 'an object' we are really talking about a plurality of appropriately connected momentary objects.

Arguably, Chisholm (1976) had something like this picture of ordinary objects. He called it the view that ordinary objects are *entia successiva:* a succession of distinct momentary objects.

There are analogues of such views elsewhere in metaphysics. For instance, suppose you are a mereological nihilist: you hold that there are no composite objects, just simples arranged in certain ways.[26] You might conclude that ordinary sentences such as 'Annie caught the ball' are false. For you might hold that such sentences could only be true if there were composite objects including Annie and a ball. But you might not draw this conclusion.[27] You might say that the sentence *appears* to quantify over two composite objects, Annie and the ball, but in fact there is disguised plural quantification. The sentence really quantifies over several pluralities of simples arranged in certain ways and is made true by there being those pluralities. This view is analogous to successionism.

So, the standard exdurantist accepts that what appear to be singular referring terms like 'Annie' and 'the statue' really are singular referring terms, but then goes on to say that contrary to what we might imagine they refer only to momentary objects. By contrast, the successionist holds, as we might expect, that these terms do not refer to momentary objects, but goes on to say that contrary to what we might have thought these terms are actually plural referring expressions.

There are two components to successionism. The first is that to *succeed* (i.e., to be a succession) involves there being a filled four-dimensional region, where that region is filled, collectively, by a bunch of momentary objects. The second involves its being the case that those momentary objects bear gen-identity relations to one another. For the successionist, what makes for the difference between there simply being a plurality of momentary objects and there being a succession is that where there is a succession there are momentary objects that bear gen-identity relations to one another.

Let's spell out this second aspect of the view. Let's say that O** is a *direct successor* of O*, iff a relation of gen-identity obtains between O** and O*. Then O* is a *successor* of O iff either O* is a direct successor of O, or there is a chain of direct successors linking O* and O. This allows that something (say O*) might be a successor of O even though there is no direct dependence between O* and O.

> **Succession**: O succeeds iff O is fully located at a four-dimensional region, R, and (i) for each M-region, M, of R there is some object that is exactly located at M; and (ii) for any two objects, O* and O**, each of which is exactly located at an M-region of R, one is a successor of the other.

Let us call someone a *successionist* if they think that actual objects succeed. On this view persistence sentences that mention 'O' are true in virtue of there

---

[26] For discussion of mereological nihilism, see van Inwagen (1990a); Parsons (2013); Sider (2013); Contessa (2014); Tallant (2014); and Rettler (2018).

[27] See Parsons (2013) for a view of this kind.

being some plurality of objects – the succession – such that: (a) 'O' picks out a plurality of objects and (b) O is fully located at a four-dimensional region and (c) the object, O*, that is exactly located at one M-region is numerically distinct from any other object, O**, that is exactly located at another M-region. On this view sentences such as 'Annie was small and fluffy' are true iff 'Annie' picks out a succession and some of that succession is located earlier than the time of utterance and has the property of being small and fluffy.

Semantic successionism is then yet another way to spell out the semantic claim.

> **Semantic successionism:** Persistence sentences are true iff (relevant) objects succeed.

Semantic successionism, like all the views we have met so far, is quite a demanding view, in that it entails that the world could seem as it does and yet persistence error theory be true. For the world could seem as it does and yet objects endure or transdure, and hence fail to succeed.

This brings us to our final view: processionism.

2.2.7 Processionism

Processionism is the view that persisting objects *proceed*. There are two components to processionism. The first is that to proceed involves being fully located at a four-dimensional region. Crucially, according to this view it does not matter *how* it is that the object is fully located at that region. So, for instance, it doesn't matter whether something is fully located at a four-dimensional region by being exactly located at each of its M-regions (as per endurantism), or by being composed of the objects that are exactly located at each M-region (as per perdurantism), or by being exactly located at the four-dimensional region at which it is fully located (as per transdurantism), or by being fully located at that region by being a plurality whose constituents jointly fill and are contained in the region (as per successionism). In *any of these cases* there is something that is fully located at the four-dimensional region and, according to the processionist, this is what matters for procession. So, according to the processionist, an object can proceed by enduring, or by perduring, or by transduring (etc.).

According to the second aspect of processionism, something proceeds only if, roughly, gen-identity relations obtain between the object at different times. Recall that an M-region is a maximally temporally unextended (i.e., three-dimensional) sub-region of a full location of an object. Each M-region corresponds to what we can think of as the region occupied by an object *at a moment of time*.

Let's introduce the locution 'O-at-M' to pick out O at an M-region. (Remember that 'O' might be a name for a succession, and hence a plurality.) Then we can talk of O-at-M_1, and O-at-M_2, and so on. We need to introduce this terminology in order to be appropriately neutral about whether there is anything exactly located at these M-regions, and, if so, whether what is exactly located at one M-region is identical to, or distinct from, what is located at any other M-region.

Let us say that O** is a *descendent* of O*, iff a relation of gen-identity obtains between O** and O*. (Recall that one way in which gen-identity relations can loosely be said to obtain between O** and O* is if the relations that ground or stand behind our P-experiences obtain between the properties of O** and O*.) Then we can say that O* is a *descendent* of O iff either O* is a direct descendent of O, or there is a chain of direct descendants linking O* and O.

Now we can say the following:

> **Proceed**: An object, O, proceeds iff (i) O is fully located at a four-dimensional region, R, and (ii) for any two M-regions in R, M*, and M**, either O-at-M* is a descendent of O-at-M** or O-at-M** is a descendent of O-at-M*.

Processionists hold that actual objects proceed. They hold that sentences such as 'Annie was small and fluffy' are true just in case 'Annie' picks out a procession, and that procession fills an earlier M-region (that is, an M-region that is earlier than the time at which we are assessing the sentence) such that Annie-at-M is small and fluffy.

With the idea of processionism in mind, we can now offer our final way of spelling out the semantic claim.

> **Semantic processionism:** Persistence sentences are true iff (relevant) objects proceed.

Notice that the first aspect of processionism – that is, that proceeding objects are fully located at four-dimensional regions – might seem reminiscent of the idea that the right answer to the question 'what is persistence?' is something like 'existing at multiple times'. For, one might think, what it is for something to be fully located at a four-dimensional region just is for that object to exist at multiple times.

That seems right. But semantic processionism tells us a lot more than just that to persist is to exist at multiple times. It tells us *what it takes* to exist at multiple times. Setting aside the second aspect of the view, it tells us that all that is required is to be fully located at a four-dimensional region. What is *not* required is that the region is filled in a particular way. So, there are lots of ways our world could be, metaphysically speaking, with respect to the ways that four-dimensional regions are filled, such that there exists a procession. They could be filled by there being something that endures, or perdures, or exdures, or succeeds. This means that the existence of any appropriate kind of enduring, perduring, or exduring of succeeding objects can make true our ordinary persistence sentences. In *this* sense, at least, semantic processionism is not very demanding: there are various ways our world could turn out to be, metaphysically speaking, such that ordinary persistence sentences come out as true. This will turn out to be important when it comes to thinking about persistence realism in Section 6.

The second aspect of processionism requires that there be relations of gen-identity. If there are no such relations then there are no processions, and according to semantic processionism our persistence sentences are not true.

So, for instance, consider the four-dimensional region that contains a momentary lemon-stage, and then a momentary plum-stage, and then a momentary grape-stage, and then a momentary peach-stage. There is something fully located at that region. We could call that object 'odd fruit'.[28] But it seems very plausible that whatever gen-identity relations turn out to be (whatever relations are in fact those which ground our P-experiences) these do not obtain between odd fruit at one time and odd fruit at any other time. If so, then according to processionism, odd fruit does not proceed even though it is fully located at a four-dimensional region. So, according to semantic processionism, the sentence 'odd fruit persists' is not true.

Is that an objection to semantic processionism? I say not.

Once we consider odd fruit, it is natural to distinguish between objects that are *temporally extended*, on the one hand, and objects that *persist*, on the other. The semantic processionist can say that odd fruit is temporally extended even though odd fruit does not persist.

At this point you might wonder: 'why think that persistence requires the existence of gen-identity relations?'. That is, why think that the right way to spell out the semantic claim includes reference to gen-identity?

You might even worry that any dispute here is merely verbal. Consider a version of processionism that simply says that to proceed is to be fully located at a four-dimensional region. Call this view *weak processionism*. The semantic processionist who accepts weak processionism (call her a *semantic weak processionist*) will say that 'odd fruit persists' is true. So, where the semantic processionist says that 'odd fruit persists' is false, but that 'odd fruit is temporally extended' is true, the semantic weak processionist says that both are true.

---

[28] For discussion of objects like odd fruit and problems they (and similar objects) might pose for perdurantists' ability to make sense of the conditions under which ordinary persistence sentences are true, see Varzi (2003) and Braddon-Mitchell and Miller (2006).

Importantly, the semantic weak processionist can still say that persistence sentences about dogs, toasters, and the like are not made true by there just being objects that are fully located at four-dimensional regions. She can say that sentences that we utter about ordinary sorts of objects are made true by processions, not weak processions; it is just that there are also some other sentences we can utter about non-ordinary things, like odd fruit, which are made true merely by there being something fully located at a four-dimensional region.

So, is the question of which view we endorse just a trivial matter? Well, remember that we are trying to fill in the semantic claim. Semantic weak processionism is the following view:

> **Semantic weak processionism:** Persistence sentences are true iff (relevant) objects weakly proceed.

Semantic weak processionism says that *all that is required* for persistence sentences to be true is that objects weakly proceed. But this is surely false. For if our world contained objects that merely weakly proceeded and did not proceed, this could only be so in virtue of there failing to be gen-identity relations. But if our world were like this, our P-experiences would be totally different from what they are. Indeed, it's not even obvious that we could have contentful mental states in such a world, given that there would be no correlation between our having certain mental states and the world being thus and so. Certainly, though, if things were like that then none of the persistence sentences that we utter or think would be true. None of our claims about dogs, or toasters, or cars, or houses, or people would be true. So semantic weak processionism is false.

Given this, let's focus on semantic processionism.

Semantic processionism entails that there are multiple ways in which an object can be extended through time such that it counts as persisting. It's a view on which succession is sufficient for persistence, but is not necessary. So, if ordinary objects succeed, then persistence error theory is false. It is also a view on which wherever we have enduring, perduring, or transduring objects, and where those objects at one time bear gen-identity relations to those objects at other times, then we have a procession. So, when endurance, perdurance, and transdurance are accompanied by the presence of gen-identity, they are also each sufficient for persistence.

Thus, if semantic processionism is true, then semantic endurantism, perdurantism, transdurantism, exdurantism, and successionism, are all false.[29]

---

[29] These five views are not the only options here. There are other views about the ways in which objects persist through time, and these could be used to construct alternative views about what persistence is. See, for instance, transcendentism, offered by Costa (2017) and Costa and Giordani (2016) and a critique by Miller (2013).

For each says that the endurance, perdurance, transdurance, exdurance, and succession (respectively) of (relevant) objects is both necessary and sufficient for persistence sentences to be true. But semantic processionism denies the necessity claim of each.

Semantic processionism is *not very demanding*. If our world is as it seems to us to be, then it will turn out that there are processions, and, in turn, it will turn out that (often) the ordinary persistence sentences that we utter and think are true. That is because if things are as they seem to us to be, then there are gen-identity relations and there are filled four-dimensional regions. For gen-identity relations just are whatever it is that our P-experiences track; we most certainly have such experiences, and we most certainly have experiences of there being filled four-dimensional regions. So, if things are as they seem to us to be, then there exist processions, and the processions that exist are the relevant ones for making true many, or most, of our ordinary persistence sentences. It doesn't matter how our world is, metaphysically speaking, with regard to whether objects endure, perdure, or something else: there are many ways our world can be, metaphysically speaking, and yet there can be (relevant) processions, and hence our persistence sentences are true.

I will argue for the claim that if our world is as it seems to us to be, then there *are* (relevant) proceeding objects, and hence persistence realism (vindicated in more detail in Sections 4, 5, and 6). This, I take it, is a mark in favour of the view: we can be relatively confident that persistence realism is true without knowing anything about the underlying metaphysical nature of our world.

Before I turn to consider such arguments, I first want to return to a consideration of how we should think about numerical identity over time in light of the views just articulated.

2.2.8 Identity over Time

As I am using the phrase 'numerical identity over time', objects are numerically identical over time only if they endure. That is because if an object endures then it is multiply located across time. We find the very same object exactly located at multiple times, and so we find a relation of numerical identity obtaining between an object exactly located at one time and an object exactly located at some other time. That is not so given any other view of persistence. But that does not mean that there is not *some* good sense in which on at least some of these views there is numerical identity over time. The most notable such view is perdurantism, though similar things can be said for transdurantism.

Consider Herbert once again. Suppose Herbert perdures. Now suppose I point to Herbert at t_3 and say, 'Herbert now is numerically identical with

Herbert at t_2'. Many perdurantists will say that what I say is true. This is despite the fact that the momentary object I point to at t_3 is numerically distinct from the momentary object that exists at t_2. How can this be? Well, the perdurantist says, when I point to Herbert at t_2 I am pointing to the whole four-dimensional object that is Herbert *by pointing to one of his parts*, and when I talk about Herbert at t_2, *I am talking about the whole four-dimensional statue* by talking about one of its parts. That four-dimensional statue is, of course, self-identical. Everything is trivially numerically identical to itself! So, in *this* sense Herbert is numerically identical over time. Herbert at t_2 is identical with Herbert now, in that at each time I am talking about one and the same four-dimensional statue.

This might seem odd. But really it is not so odd. After all, we are talking about a statue, Herbert. But most of us (exdurantists excluded) think that statues are, by their very nature, temporally extended. There are no instantaneous statues! So, if we are talking about Herbert, we must be talking about the four-dimensional object. It's hard to point to that object at any moment of time, since at that moment all that is in front of us is a temporal part of Herbert. Nonetheless, we *are* pointing to the four-dimensional object, since we are intending to point to Herbert himself, not just to a part of him. Think about when you see someone you know, and you point him or her out to a friend. 'There is Jemima', you say, pointing at Jemima's head or chest. No one is tempted to think that you are in fact picking out a head (or chest) and saying that *that* is Jemima. We point to a part of Jemima, and in doing so we pick out and talk about all of her.

The transdurantist will say something similar: namely, that we are picking out the whole four-dimensional object when we point to, or talk about, that object at a given time.

In neither case do I think this is well captured by saying that these are views on which there is numerical identity over time.

Instead, let's introduce the idea of *singular reference*. Singular reference occurs when we use some expression, at multiple times, to pick out one and the same object. The endurantist secures singular reference by holding that although when we pick out an enduring object at a given time, we pick out something that is three-dimensional – something that is exactly located at an M-region – we pick out the *very same object* at another time because the object that is exactly located at that later time is numerically identical with the object that is exactly located at the earlier time. While perdurantists and transdurantists deny that there is any numerical identity over time, they can still secure singular reference. They do so by denying that when we pick out an object at a given time we pick out something that is three-dimensional. Instead, they hold that we pick out a four-dimensional object and that we pick out *the same* four-dimensional object at other times. (By contrast, the successionist says that these are not cases of singular reference at all; instead, they are cases of plural reference. Still, she will say that we pick out the *same* plurality, at different times, with an expression like 'Annie'.)

2.2.9 Recap

Let's recap. In order to determine whether persistence error theory or persistence realism is true, we need to know what it would take for persistence sentences to be true. Once we know this, we can turn to consider what our world is like, to see if our world is one that makes those sentences true. So, the first stage of investigation involves *semantic* investigation, while the second stage of investigation involves *ontological* investigation. So far, I have engaged in the first of these investigations by presenting different ways of spelling out the semantic claim. I've introduced six different views about the conditions under which persistence sentences are true. In Sections 4 and 5 I argue in favour of one of these accounts: semantic processionism. But first, I want to return to persistence error theory. After all, many philosophers have rejected such a view out of hand, which suggests that perhaps we don't need to come up with fancy arguments in favour of persistence realism! In what follows I want to say a bit more about why I think we should at least take persistence error theory seriously, by saying a bit more about what such a view might look like.

3 Persistence Error Theory

In this section I consider two arguments against persistence error theory. I will try to show that neither of these is very compelling. In doing so, I will say a bit more about what persistence error theory might look like. None of this means that I endorse persistence error theory: it just means that I think we should recognise, and set aside, *these* arguments against error theory and in favour of realism.

3.1 The Argument from Semantic Externalism

I will call the first argument against persistence error theory *the argument from semantic externalism*.

Persistence error theory is true just in case most ordinary persistence sentences fail to be true. Whether a persistence sentence is true or not depends, of course, on what that sentence means. But there is a lot of disagreement in the philosophy of language regarding meaning.

Those who are broadly *semantic internalists* think that the meanings of words are determined by factors internal to speakers, and hence that each of us has some (perhaps imperfect) access to what our words mean. Internalists often think that reflection on the situations in which we are inclined to use those terms gives us some access to their meanings.[30]

By contrast, *semantic externalists* think that some, or all, of the meanings of terms is determined by factors external to the speaker.[31] Common versions of these views hold that, very roughly, the meanings of our terms are governed by what it is in the world to which our use of those terms is appropriately causally connected. So, for instance, suppose the term 'water' is introduced to pick out the watery drinkable stuff around here that we are causally in contact with (i.e., the stuff we drink and bathe in) and we use that term in a way that is sensitive to the presence of that watery stuff. Now suppose that this watery stuff turns out to be H_2O. Then it is part of the meaning of 'water' that it refers to H_2O, and that was so even before we came to know the chemical composition of the watery stuff. Hence, we can be ignorant of the meanings of our terms since we can be ignorant of that component of meaning that is external to speakers.

Many philosophers these days are semantic externalists of one kind or another. This suggests one route to rejecting persistence error theory right from the outset. Here is the idea. Clearly there are objects to which our various persistence expressions are causally connected. For instance, in our house we introduced the name 'Annie' to pick out a certain black labradoodle over time. Given the way we introduced the name, it seems trivial that the name refers, and that it refers to something that persists. Hence, it seems to be trivial that 'Annie persists' is true. We can tell a similar story for other persistence sentences. So, based on this sort of reasoning we can conclude that persistence error theory is false. While we can certainly learn something about the *nature* of persistence, we are not going to learn that persistence error theory is true. And if this is right it would vindicate the orthodox philosophical view that we should be focussing on *how* objects persist, not on *whether* they do.

This argument, however, fails. To see why, we need only notice that *all* our terms are causally connected in some way or other with certain bits of the world. There was *something* in the world that was causally connected to people making utterances about witches. The semantic externalist does not, however, want to

---

[30] See Loar (1976); Lewis (1984); Kroon (1987); Jackson (1998(a), 1998(b), 2004, 2009, 2007); Jackson and Chalmers (2001); Braddon-Mitchell (2004); Chalmers (2004); and Braddon-Mitchell and Nola (2009). Descriptivism, in this sense, is a broad view that incorporates causal descriptivism on which causal claims can be (and often are) part of the referencing fixing description and it also includes views like two-dimensional semantics on which terms have multiple intensions, one (the primary or A-intension) that is basically a referencing fixing description, and the other (the secondary or C-intension) that is the intension that takes us to the actual extension.

[31] Defenders of this kind of approach include Kripke (1980); Salmon (1983); Soames (1987, 2002, 2004); Devitt (1991); and King (2001).

say that there really are (or were) witches. In general, the externalist does not want to make error theory impossible. Externalists typically respond to these kinds of problems by suggesting that there are *reference fixing descriptions*: these are the things that 'fix the reference' of our term (that is, pick out something in the world, or not) and then allow us to examine the nature of that thing, which will, in turn, tell us what our terms mean. The reference fixing description is that description which allows us to work out *what* to test in order to work out that water is H_2O.

The reference fixing description is part of what fixes the meaning even though it's not part of the meaning itself. So, the thought goes, error theory about witches turned out to be true because the reference fixing description associated with 'witch' did not pick out anything in the world. Perhaps, for instance, the reference fixing description included the fact that witches are supernatural, or that they have magical powers, or that they cavort with the devil. Since nothing was like this, there turned out to be nothing to which 'witch' referred. Hence, there was no external aspect of meaning to be discovered.

But given this, it remains a possibility that the reference fixing description for various ordinary expressions like 'Annie' and 'Herbert' and 'persists' are also such that those expressions turn out to fail to pick out anything in the world. If it is part of the reference fixing description for 'Annie' that there exists something which is numerically identical over time, for instance, then it could still be that persistence error theory is true since there could fail to be any such thing. So, while persistence error theory may well turn out to be false, we do not learn that it is false just by endorsing semantic externalism.

3.2 The Argument from Unthinkability

That brings us to a second argument against persistence error theory. Call this the *unthinkability argument*. According to the unthinkability argument, persistence error theory must be false. Our very way of being in the world presupposes that there are persisting objects. Nothing that we do makes any sense if this is not so. If we are not persisting objects then it makes no sense for us to claim to remember what we did in the past, or to be held responsible for any past actions; it makes no sense to deliberate about what we will do in the future, or to anticipate any future events. Likewise, none of our interpersonal relationships make any sense since our engagement with others is almost always bound up with our taking those others to be persisting objects with whom we have already interacted and will interact in the future. So, the argument proceeds, the idea that we, and those around us, do not persist is unthinkable. For this reason, it must be that objects persist.

The error theorist, however, can respond to this kind of argument. One possibility is that she could endorse some version of *persistence fictionalism*.[32] Very roughly, persistence fictionalism is the view that persistence *sentences* are literally false (persistence error theory is true) but persistence *discourse* is not. So, persistence fictionalists try to show that our persistence discourse is in good standing even though persistence sentences are literally false.

How could this be? According to the fictionalist, when we utter persistence sentences we are not asserting the literal content of those sentences. Instead, we are either asserting some non-literal content of those sentences, or we are not asserting their content at all; rather, we are expressing some other sort of attitude towards them.

The first option is *object persistence fictionalism*.[33] This is the view that although persistence sentences are false, when we utter those sentences we don't say false things because we don't assert the literal content of those sentences. For example, when I utter 'it is raining cats and dogs' I am not asserting the literal content of that sentence. If I were, I would be asserting something false since there are in fact no cats or dogs falling from the sky. Instead, I am asserting some non-literal content; namely, that it is raining very hard. And *that* assertion can be true, and indeed will be true just in case it is indeed raining very hard. So, according to the object persistence fictionalist, when we utter persistence sentences we are asserting some content other than their literal content, and *that* content is true.

By analogy, consider the mereological nihilist. She says there are no composite objects, and hence there is no composite object, Annie the labradoodle. Let's suppose she says that, given this, sentences such as 'Annie is a labradoodle' are strictly speaking false. Still, there are simples arranged Annie-wise. If there *were* composition, there being simples arranged Annie-wise *would* be sufficient for sentences such as 'Annie is a labradoodle' to be true. That is, *in the fiction of composition* its being the case that there are simples arranged that way entails that composite object Annie exists. So, she might say, when we utter sentences such as 'Annie is a labradoodle' we are in fact asserting that things are as they would be required to be, in the fiction, for 'Annie is a labradoodle' to be true that is, we are asserting that there are simples arranged Annie-wise which are also arranged labradoodle-wise, and that is true.

The object persistence fictionalist can say something very similar. She can hold that *in the persistence fiction*, the world being as it seems to us to be

---

[32] In particular, the view I have in mind is hermeneutic fictionalism, which is a claim about the right interpretation of our current discourse (rather than a claim about revising our discourse in some manner).

[33] For discussion of different versions of fictionalism, see Yablo (2001).

(roughly speaking) would make (literally) true, our persistence sentences. Those sentences are in fact false (since the fiction does not obtain), but when we assert these sentences we are in fact asserting that the world is as it seems to us to be, and since by and large the world is this way, by and large those sentences are true.

So, according to the object fictionalist, 'Herbert persists' is true if and only if δ, and δ is not the case. Perhaps the object fictionalist endorses semantic endurantism, and she thinks that 'Herbert persists' is true only if there is an enduring statue, while in fact there is not. So, the sentence is false. Yet, says the object fictionalist, when any of us utters 'Herbert persists' we are best interpreted not as asserting the literal content of that sentence, and hence asserting a falsehood, but rather as asserting the non-literal content of that sentence: namely, that our world seems to us to be a certain way with respect to statue-shaped objects at times that is, it seems as though there are such objects, at times, and that they bear certain similarity and causal relations to one another – and in the persistence fiction the world being that way is a world in which objects endure, and hence a world in which the sentence is literally true. Since our world does indeed seem to be one in which there are statue-like objects, at times, that bear certain similarity and causal relations to one another, the non-literal content of the sentence we assert is true. Hence, we assert a truth. Thus, our persistence discourse is in good standing.

Other persistence error theorists might endorse other versions of persistence fictionalism. For instance, the persistence fictionalist might endorse *pretence persistence fictionalism*. Then she will say that persistence sentences are false, but that we do not assert the literal content of those sentences when we utter them. Instead, we are not in fact *asserting* anything at all; we are expressing some non-cognitive attitude (that is, an attitude that is not a belief, such as a desire, or a hope, or a dread) towards the content of those sentences. In particular, she might say that we are *pretending* that they are true. Hence our utterances are not false, since they are not truth-apt. That is, they are not apt to be either true or false, because only beliefs are apt to be true or false: a hope, or desire, or indeed a pretence, cannot be true or false. So, once again, our persistence discourse is in good standing even though persistence sentences are false, because what we are doing when we engage in that discourse is not asserting the literal content of the sentences that we utter. Indeed, we are not asserting any content at all. We are doing something entirely different: we are pretending that those sentences are true. Hence the fact that the literal content of those sentences is false is irrelevant to whether our persistence discourse is in good standing since we are not asserting that content.

Interestingly, little consideration has been given to these views, and that's a pity. These sorts of fictionalism avoid, or at least appear to avoid, the worry that persistence error theory is unthinkable. For it leaves our persistence discourse in good standing.

So, I do not think that persistence error theory can be discarded on these grounds. Rather, I think that persistence error theory turns out to be false because the right analysis of the conditions under which persistence sentences are true is one on which they come out as true if, roughly, our world is as it seems to us to be. And that is why we can be confident that those sentences are true without knowing how it is that objects persist.

Next, I begin, in Section 4, by arguing for the plausibility of semantic processionism as an account of the conditions under which persistence sentences are true. To do this, I try to show that our judgements about when such sentences are true, and when they are false, nicely align with semantic processionism rather than the competitor views. After having considered some objections to semantic processionism in Section 5, I then move on to argue, in Section 6, that if semantic processionism is true then we can be confident that most of the ordinary persistence sentences that we take to be true are indeed true. Hence persistence realism will be vindicated.

4 Semantic Processionism

According to semantic processionism, it is both necessary and sufficient that there are (relevant) processions for persistence sentences to be true. To show that semantic processionism is a plausible view, then, we need to show that each of these claims (necessity and sufficiency) is plausible. I begin with sufficiency (Section 4.1) and then move on to necessity (Section 4.2).

4.1 The Sufficiency of Processions

In what follows I offer two arguments for the sufficiency of processions for persistence (henceforth just the sufficiency of procession). The first is the argument from access.

The Argument from Access[34]

(1) We can tell that often ordinary persistence sentences are true.
(2) We can only tell that often ordinary persistence sentences are true if we can tell that there are persisting objects.

---

[34] I use continuous numbering of premises to be able to refer to each premise (or conclusion) with a unique number.

(3) We can tell that there are persisting objects only if we can tell that we can reliably detect persisting objects.

(4) We can tell that we can reliably detect persisting objects only if procession is sufficient for persistence.

(5) Therefore, procession is sufficient for persistence.

The first thing to say about this argument is that it is framed in terms of what we can *tell*. Here, I am thinking of being able to tell something as being aware of that thing, or being aware that one can detect that thing. We can distinguish 'being able to tell' that something is the case, from *knowing* that it is the case. Many philosophers are externalists about knowledge. For instance, reliabilists think that, very roughly, I know that P just in case I believe P, and I am able reliably to detect that P. Importantly, even if I can in fact reliably detect that P, I might not be *aware* that I can reliably detect that P. I might not be able to *tell* that I can reliably detect P. What makes such a view externalist, then, is that even though it might be true of me that I know P, I might not be in a position to *tell* that I know P.

So, for instance, suppose that there are in fact auras, and I am in fact a reliable detector of those auras. But suppose that I have no way of telling that I am reliably detecting auras. For all I am aware, it might be that I am simply having peculiar visual presentations. It could be, as far as I am aware, that I am not reliably detecting anything at all. Then, while I might, on some accounts of knowledge, count as knowing that there is an aura there (if I believe that there is and I have reliably detected it), I won't be able to *tell* that I know this.

With this in mind, I think (1) is plausible. We can, I say, tell that many persistence sentences are true. Premise (2) is also plausible. On the assumption that persistence sentences are about persisting objects, and so are true only if there are persisting objects, we can tell that ordinary persistence sentences are true only if we can tell that there are persisting objects (and indeed, the right objects to make those sentences true).

In turn, (3) is pretty compelling. How can I tell that there are persisting objects of the right kinds to make ordinary persistence sentences true? Well, I can do so only if I can tell that I can reliably detect there being such objects. If I could not tell whether I can reliably detect persisting objects, then I could not tell that there *are* such objects.

Here is why we should accept (4). First, we *can* reliably detect processions. We can detect whether there are four-dimensional regions at which something is fully located, and we can detect whether there are gen-identity relations between the object(s) that are located at the M-regions of such four-dimensional regions. That is because, as I noted earlier, gen-identity relations are just whatever relation or relations it is that we are tracking, or which ground, our having

P-experiences. Since there surely is something in our world that we are tracking when we have such experiences (even if it's just a sort of pattern in the distributions of things) we can tell that there are gen-identity relations.

Moreover, not only can we reliably detect processions, we can tell that we reliably detect them. That is, we have good access to the fact that we reliably detect them. That is because we have good access to the fact that we have P-experiences. Indeed, it's hard to see how we could be wrong about having such experiences.

So, we can tell that we can reliably detect processions.

Now, at this point you might say: but suppose that in fact the processions around here endure. So, when we are detecting processions *we are thereby detecting enduring objects*. Hence, if it's true that we can reliably detect processions, then it's also true that we can reliably detect enduring objects. Similar considerations apply if objects transdure or perdure. Hence, while it's true that we can detect persisting objects if they proceed, it's also true that we can detect them if they endure or perdure or transdure. So (4) is false.

It's true that if the processions in our world endure, then we can reliably detect enduring objects. Can we, though, *tell* that we are detecting persisting objects? Well, if persisting objects just are processions then we can, since we can tell that we can reliably detect processions. But can we tell whether we can reliably detect *enduring* objects? No. After all, the world would seem the same to us whether the processions we are reliably detecting endure or perdure (etc.). So, even if we were reliably detecting enduring objects, we would not be in a position to tell that that is what we were doing. As far as we can tell, it could just as easily be that we were detecting perduring objects, or transduring objects.

The point is this. If semantic endurantism were true, for instance, and processions were not sufficient for persistence because endurance is necessary, then we could not tell that we were in fact detecting enduring objects even if in fact we were. For we could not tell whether the processions that we are reliably detecting *do in fact endure*. We would have no way of detecting whether the persistence sentences that we take to be true are in fact true, and hence (4) would be false.

Likewise, suppose that in fact the processions that we are reliably detecting are in fact perduring objects. Then we do in fact reliably detect perduring objects by detecting processions. But if procession is not sufficient for persistence and, instead, perdurance is necessary, can we tell that we are detecting persisting objects? No. For we cannot determine whether we are in fact detecting perduring objects. After all, the world could seem just as it does to us and there be no perduring objects, because instead there are enduring objects, or transduring objects. So, even if we were detecting perduring objects, we could not *tell* that we were doing so, and so it would not be true that we can tell that persistence sentences are true.

In general, what makes it possible for us to tell that we are reliably detecting persisting objects is that semantic processionism is relatively undemanding. It doesn't require that the objects in our world have a particular metaphysical nature – endurance, or perdurance, or transdurance – for persistence sentences to be true. This is important, since while these underlying metaphysical natures might be detectable, we are unable to tell which nature it is that we are detecting! So, if detecting these natures, and being able to tell that we detect them, is required for us to be able to tell that persistence sentences are true, then it won't be true that we can tell that they are true. That is why we can only tell that such sentences are true if semantic processionism is true. Hence (4) is true.

Here is a second argument.

The Argument from Care

(6) Our persistence discourse is such that persisting objects are those things towards which we sometimes direct diachronic care.

(7) We direct diachronic care towards processions.

(8) Therefore, our persistence discourse is such that procession is sufficient for persistence.

By diachronic care, I mean the kind of care that we direct over time. It's care that is sensitive to what has been, and will be, the case: it's not the kind of care that any of us can direct towards a momentary thing. I lovingly have my car serviced because it's the same car I have been driving for ten years. I care about this particular dog because he is Freddie, the same labradoodle that I have been living with for seven years. This is diachronic care.

Our persistence discourse is riddled with persistence sentences about diachronic care. It's fair to say that this discourse is one in which persisting things are often (certainly sometimes) the things towards which we direct this kind of care. When we ask what persistence is, it seems natural to say that it's the kind of thing that 'stands behind' and rationalises our having this kind of pattern of diachronic care. It would be very surprising if someone came up with an account of persistence such that the objects towards which we direct diachronic care, and the objects that persist, turned out to be two entirely different sets of objects. A natural response to such an account would be to think that, whatever it's an account of, it's not an account of persistence at all: for these two things should go together. So, we should accept (6).

Premise (7) is true. Diachronic care is directed towards processions. First, this is because it is processions that we can tell that we are detecting. We certainly do not diachronically care about things we cannot detect. Moreover, I think it's plausible that we do not diachronically care about things whose detection we cannot be confident of: things we cannot tell that we detect. I cannot tell if I am detecting enduring or perduring objects. So it seems very odd to think that the reason that I care about those things is because they endure or perdure, that I care about them qua enduring or perduring object.

To put it another way, in ordinary circumstances we care about our nearest and dearest, and we do so, I say, regardless of whether they endure, or perdure, or transdure (etc.). I would not somehow care less about Freddie if I came to learn that Freddie does not (say) endure. And that is because, I say, it is processions that we care about. That is why learning that a particular procession about which I care, does not endure, or does not perdure, or does not transdure, makes *no difference* to the quality of my care. For I was not caring about that thing qua enduring thing, or qua perduring thing: I was caring about it qua proceeding thing.

So, if persisting objects are those about which we (at least sometimes) diachronically care, and if we diachronically care about processions, then it must be sufficient, for something to persist, that it proceeds. Hence (8) is true.

This ends the arguments for the claim that procession is sufficient for persistence. Notably, if procession is sufficient for persistence, then the competing semantic views are false. Semantic endurantism says that endurance is necessary for persistence; but that cannot be true if procession is sufficient, since some processions do not endure. Semantic perdurantism says that perdurance is necessary for persistence; but that cannot be true if procession is sufficient, since some processions do not perdure. Semantic transdurantism says that transdurance is necessary for persistence; but that cannot be true if procession is sufficient, since some processions do not transdure. Semantic successionism says that succession is necessary for persistence; but that cannot be true if procession is sufficient, since some processions do not succeed.

That brings us to the necessity claim.

4.2 Semantic Processionism: The Necessity Claim

Why think that processions must exist in order for ordinary persistence sentences to be true? Here is an argument to that conclusion.

The Necessity of Processions

(9) If we judge that worlds that fail to contain processions are worlds in which ordinary persistence sentences are not true, then this is good

evidence that processions are necessary for ordinary persistence sentences to be true.

(10) We judge that worlds that fail to contain processions are worlds in which ordinary persistence sentences are not true.

(11) Therefore, there is good evidence that processions are necessary for ordinary persistence sentences to be true.

Consider premise (9). Semantic internalists like myself should find (9) plausible. If you think that it is the contents of our heads (so to speak) that determine the meanings of terms, then you are likely to think that we have at least some, defeasible access to the meanings of our terms. Moreover, you are very likely to think that we can get access to at least certain aspects of the meanings of our terms by looking at the various conditions under which we are inclined to use, and not use, those terms.

Semantic externalists, though, might baulk at (9). After all, they think that at least part of the meaning of our terms is given by things external to the head, and hence that we can be ignorant of what our terms mean. Still, as I noted earlier, in Section 3.1, even externalists grant that we have access to some kind of reference-fixing description which allows us to find 'samples' of things in the world (like water or dogs), so that by investigating those things we can figure out what our terms mean. So, even semantic externalists will concede that if the reference-fixing description we have for terms like 'persistence' and 'dog' and so on are such that there simply are no samples of those things to examine in a world, then it will turn out that those terms fail to refer, and that sentences that say of those things that they exist will fail to be true. If we are inclined to judge those scenarios that lack processions as being ones in which ordinary persistence sentences are not true, this gives us reason to think that the reference-fixing description for the relevant terms/expressions is one that mentions processions, and hence that in the absence of any processions those sentences will fail to be true. So, we should accept (9).

What of premise (10)? Consider a scenario in which objects are fully located at four-dimensional regions, but these objects do not proceed because there are no gen-identity relations (or chains thereof) between those objects at one time and those objects at any other time. That scenario seems to be one in which none of our ordinary persistence sentences are true. In this scenario there is no stability or projectability of things over time precisely because how things are, at later times, has nothing whatever to do with how they were at earlier times. And that would surely be a scenario in which none of the persistence sentences that we take to be true, come out as true.

At this point you might object. Perhaps in the scenario just described our ordinary persistence sentences would indeed be false. But suppose it were to turn out that our world is as it seems to us to be, *but there are no processions*. Perhaps *then* we would still judge that most of the persistence sentences we take to be true are in fact true. And if we would judge that, then we have reason to think that semantic processionism is false. While it might be that the presence of processions is sufficient for our persistence sentences to be true, they would not turn out to be necessary.

The response to this objection should already be obvious. Our world could not seem to us just as it does, and yet there be no processions.

So, we should conclude that (10) is true. The presence of processions is necessary for persistence sentences to be true because there being processions doesn't really require that much. If there aren't processions then persistence sentences won't be true because it won't even be the case that there are counterfactual dependencies obtaining between earlier and later objects.

If, however, semantic processionism is true, then what this tells us is that almost all the candidate semantic analyses offered in Section 2 are inadequate. Surprisingly, they provide neither necessary *nor* sufficient conditions for persistence sentences to be true. One might have thought that even if endurance, perdurance, transdurance, or succession is *necessary* for persistence, nevertheless each of them is sufficient. That is so, however, only if endurance, perdurance, transdurance, and succession each entail procession. In what follows I will argue that this is false when it comes to endurance, perdurance, and transdurance.

Consider, first, perdurance. Recall that we defined perdurance as follows:

> **Perdure**: An object, O, perdures iff O is exactly located at a four-dimensional region, R, and for each M-region of R, there is a temporal part of O that is exactly located at that M-region.

This definition tells us that something perdures iff it is exactly located at a four-dimensional region and has temporal parts at each M-region of that region. But nothing about this entails that the various temporal parts bear gen-identity relations to one another. Consider Annie and Freddie (both labra-doodles – Annie is black and Freddie is cream if it helps with visualisation). Now consider the four-dimensional object that is composed of Annie-at-t_1 (an instantaneous temporal part of Annie), Freddie-at-t_2 (an instantaneous temporal part of Freddie), Annie-at-t_3, Freddie-at-t_4, (and so on). The resulting object – call it AF – is exactly located at a four-dimensional region, R, and for each M-region of R, there is a temporal part of AF that is exactly located at that M-region. So given our definition above, AF perdures. AF does not, however, proceed. AF meets clause (i) of our definition of procession: it is fully located at a four-dimensional regional R (by being exactly located at it). But it doesn't meet clause (ii).

Now, the perdurantist could amend her definition of perdurance to something like the following:

> **Perdure***: An object, O, perdures iff O is exactly located at a four-dimensional region, R, and for each M-region of R, there is an object, O*, that is exactly located at that M-region such that for any two objects, O* and O**, which are exactly located at M-regions of O, O* and O** are (a) proper parts of O and (b) either O** is a descendent of O* or O* is a descendent of O**.

Then it will follow that perduring objects proceed, and so the necessity of processions for persistence will be consistent with the sufficiency of perdurance for persistence.

The resulting view is consistent with holding that composition itself is unrestricted: namely, that for any x and y, there is something that is composed of x and y.[35] One could hold that there are many 'temporally extended' four-dimensional objects: namely, those objects that are composed of objects that are exactly located at various three-dimensional regions. But many (and indeed most) of these will not *perdure* since they will not proceed. Given this amended version of perdurantism it will turn out that if semantic processionism is true, then perdurance is sufficient for persistence even though it is not necessary.

Exactly similar considerations arise in the context of standard exdurantism, so I will not rehearse those here.

Now consider endurance. Recall we defined endurance as follows:

> **Endure**: An object, O, endures iff O is fully located at a four-dimensional region, R, and O is exactly located at each M-region in R.

Again, there is nothing about this definition (at least on the face of it) that entails that enduring objects proceed. That is because there seems to be nothing that would prevent an object being multiply located, and yet it being the case that the object at one location fails to be gen-identity related to the object at some other location. Such objects would endure, but not proceed. If so, then, conditional on semantic processionism being true, it follows that endurance is not sufficient for procession, and hence not sufficient for persistence either.

At this point friends of endurance might demur. They might argue that what it is for an object to endure is for there to be *immanent causation* over time. Immanent causation is to be contrasted with *transeunt causation*. Transeunt

---

[35] Defenders of unrestricted composition include Lewis (1986); Heller (1990); Sider (2001, 2003); and Miller (2006b). By contrast, those who defend some version of restricted composition include van Inwagen (1990a); Merricks (2001); and Markosian (2008).

causation is causation that occurs between distinct objects (as when Freddie gnaws a bone, thus causing it to have teeth marks). Immanent causation is causation in which the way an object is at one time is the causal result of the way it is at some earlier time. Viewed this way, immanent causation looks a lot like gen-identity. If objects endure, then we would expect that what underlies gen-identity will be relations between the *properties* of enduring objects at given times. After all, substantive existential dependence relations are asymmetric. So, if x depends on y, then y does not depend on x. Identity is symmetric. So, it is not obvious how O at t* can be identical with O at t, and yet it be the case that O at t* existentially depends on O at t. Better, then, to say that the dependence obtains between the properties of O at different times. If immanent causation is causation in which the way an object is at one time is the causal result of the way it is at some earlier time, then it is plausible that where there is immanent causation there is also gen-identity. So, if endurance entails that there are immanent causal relations between an enduring object at one time, and at other times (or chains thereof), then it also seems to entail that there are relations of gen-identity between the enduring object at one time, and at other times (or chains thereof).

If this is right, then it would show that given the truth of semantic procession-ism endurance *is* sufficient for procession, and hence persistence, even though it's not necessary.

How might we try to show that if O endures, then O at one time bears gen-identity relations (or chains thereof) to O at any other time? One possibility would be to offer an analysis, or perhaps a reduction, of diachronic numerical identity to relations of gen-identity. If diachronic numerical identity simply *consists* in the obtaining of such relations, then it would follow that endurance entails procession.

I think this idea is problematic. First, I take numerical identity to be both *fundamental* and *primitive*. Numerical identity is primitive if it cannot be explicated in other terms. If numerical identity is primitive, then although we can say some interesting and useful things to illuminate that notion (as Leibniz does), we cannot *define* numerical identity in any other terms. Numerical identity is fundamental if it does not supervene on, or reduce to, facts about anything else. If so, there is no answer to the question 'in virtue of what is x self-identical?'.[36]

If numerical identity is fundamental there might still be important questions about identity that have sensible answers. One might ask: why is Clark Kent identical with Superman? And there might be a sensible answer to that question

---

[36] See Erica Shumener (2020) for a view to the contrary.

which is along the following lines: because they are both just different names for the same alien chap, but he received the name Clark Kent from his adopted human parents and the name 'Superman' as a name for the Lycra-wearing superhero he is. This is a useful thing to know. But it's not an answer to the question of why something is self-identical; it's an answer to a question about why certain names co-refer, or why it is that one thing has two names.[37]

If identity is both fundamental and primitive then we cannot analyse identity in terms of the obtaining of relations of gen-identity, nor can we reduce identity to the obtaining of gen-identity relations. And if that is right, then there seems no reason to think that the presence of numerical identity is always accompanied by relations of gen-identity. In turn, there seems no reason to think that, of necessity, enduring objects proceed, and hence no reason to think that endurance is sufficient for persistence.

Suppose, though, you deny that identity is fundamental and primitive. Might you then be able to offer a reduction of identity to gen-identity? Well, that depends what gen-identity relations turn out to consist in. Suppose they at least partly consist in sui generis existential dependence relations. Then the prospects for a reduction are bad indeed. For, as just noted, identity is a symmetric relation and existential dependence relations are asymmetric. Since no symmetric relation is asymmetric, it follows trivially that identity cannot be reduced to gen-identity.

But perhaps it might turn out that gen-identity relations are symmetric. Then, at least in theory, such a reduction would be possible, but only at the cost of having a disjunctive analysis. Suppose we say that what it is for x to be numerically identical with y is for x to bear relations of gen-identity to y (or, perhaps, for x to either bear a gen-identity relation to y, or to bear a chain of gen-identity relations that connect x with y). That clearly will not do as an analysis. After all, consider an object that exists for a single moment. Call it Shorty. Shorty is self-identical. But Shorty does not bear a gen-identity relation to any z. So, this cannot be an analysis of numerical identity, *simpliciter*.

Now, you might think that there's a more complex analysis to be had. For instance, you might argue that diachronic numerical identity is to be analysed in terms of relations of gen-identity, while synchronic numerical identity is not. That will require that you distinguish two kinds of identity and then offer a disjunctive analysis of identity itself, such that x is numerically identical with y iff either (a) (an analysis of synchronic identity) or (b) (an analysis of diachronic identity). Any such account is becoming rather baroque and, to my mind, unattractive.

---

[37] Merricks (1999b) makes a related point in the context of personal identity.

Even if none of this bothered us, however, this sort of analysis of diachronic identity just doesn't look very plausible. I can easily imagine that relations of gen-identity obtain between distinct objects. (Successionism might be false, but it's not conceptually or metaphysically confused.) The presence of such relations between objects at given times cannot be sufficient for there to be an enduring object, and so we cannot analyse endurance in terms of such relations.

So far, then, we have found no good reason to think that endurance entails procession, and hence no good reason to think that endurance is sufficient for persistence (if semantic processionism is true).

Another option would be to argue that endurance entails procession because there is a necessary connection between the two, even though diachronic identity is not to be analysed in terms of gen-identity. I really don't see why such a necessary connection should obtain. Perhaps the endurantist can come up with a compelling account of why there is such a connection. If she can, it will follow that endurance is sufficient, but not necessary, for persistence. If not, then endurance will be neither necessary nor sufficient for persistence.

Is it plausible that, in the absence of endurance entailing procession, endurance is not sufficient for persistence? If it is not, then this would be a good reason to suspect that semantic processionism is false.

Well, suppose it turned out that in our world there exists the following enduring object M. M is the table-at-M_1 (a three-dimensional thing that looks like a table at M_1), which is numerically identical with the ball-at-M_2 (a three-dimensional thing that looks like a ball at M_2). M is multiply located, first at M_1, and then at M_2. First, it looks like a table, and then later, it looks like a ball. M is not a procession: there is no gen-identity relation between the table-at-M_1 and the ball-at-M_2.

The first thing to say, here, is that if our world only contained objects like M, then our ordinary persistence sentences would be false. So, the presence of enduring objects that are not processions is not sufficient to render our ordinary persistence sentences true. That is why semantic endurantism is false.

Still, you might wonder whether, if our world contained processions that do make our ordinary persistence sentences true, and our world also contained M, we would conclude that M does not persist. The semantic processionist is committed to saying that M does not persist, since M does not proceed. I am not troubled by this; I am inclined to say that M does not persist. M is relevantly like odd fruit: it's temporally extended, because it is fully located at a four-dimensional region. But it doesn't persist. The reason I find this plausible is because I think that persistence just is the thing that you and I talk about when we utter ordinary persistence sentences, and none of our ordinary persistence sentences is about anything remotely like M. So, while M is an interesting metaphysical curiosity, it doesn't persist.

Moving on, it is also the case that if semantic processionism is true, then transdurance is not sufficient for persistence.

Recall our definition of transdurance.

> **Transdure**: An object, O, transdures iff O is exactly located at a four-dimensional region, R, and there is no object, O*, that is exactly located at any M-region of O which is a part of O.

Again, nothing about this definition requires that a transduring object is such that at each M-region it is gen-identity related to itself at each other M-region. Again, we could amend the definition in a similar manner to that of the perdurantist, to make it the case that transduring objects are processions. (I leave this as a job for the reader.) If we do that then, according to semantic processionism, transdurance will be sufficient, but not necessary, for persistence.

Finally, consider successionism.

> **Succession**: O succeeds iff O is fully located at a four-dimensional region, R, and (i) for each M-region, M, of R, there is some object that is exactly located at M; and (ii) for any two objects, O* and O**, each of which is exactly located at an M-region of R, either O* is a successor of O** or O** is a successor of O*

If an object succeeds, then it proceeds: clause (ii) of the definition tells us that. So, if semantic processionism is true, then succession is sufficient, but not necessary, for persistence.

In this section I've argued for the necessity component of semantic processionism: namely, that processions are necessary for persistence. Our persistence sentences are true only if there exist processions. On the assumption that objects can perdure, endure, transdure, or exdure without proceeding, it follows that perdurance, endurance, transdurance, and exdurance are not sufficient for persistence. In what follows I take up several objections to semantic processionism and attempt to respond to them.

5 Objections to Semantic Processionism

Here is a sort of master argument against semantic processionism.

The Master Argument

(12) According to semantic processionism, procession is both necessary and sufficient for persistence.

(13) The presence of an enduring/perduring/transduring procession is not sufficient for persistence.

(14) Therefore, semantic processionism is false.

Semantic processionists hold that: (a) enduring proceeding objects persist; (b) perduring proceeding objects persist; (c) transduring proceeding objects persist; and (d) successions persist.

This potentially leaves the semantic processionist open to arguments on several fronts. For endurantists have mounted arguments against perdurantism, and perdurantists have mounted arguments against endurantism, and transdurantists have mounted arguments against perdurantism, and so on. Many of these arguments can be marshalled against (a), (b), or (c) above, and hence against semantic processionism.

In what follows I will articulate some of these arguments and respond on the part of the semantic processionist. I begin with the version of the master argument that focusses on perduring processions (Section 5.1) before turning to the version that focusses on enduring processions (Section 5.2).

5.1 Against the Persistence of Perduring Processions

Here is the first version of the master argument.

Master Argument: Perdurantist Version

(15) According to semantic processionism, the presence of a perduring procession is sufficient for persistence (semantic processionism).
(16) The presence of a perduring procession is not sufficient for persistence.
(17) Therefore, semantic processionism is false.

Premise (15) is true, so we can focus entirely on premise (16). In what follows I consider and reject an argument for (16).

The Argument from Change

(16.1) Perduring processions are sufficient for persistence only if the presence of perduring processions makes true most of the ordinary persistence sentences that we take to be true (semantic processionism).
(16.2) Most of the ordinary persistence sentences that we take to be true are true only if ordinary objects change over time.
(16.3) If ordinary objects are perduring processions, then they do not change over time.
(16.4) Therefore, if ordinary objects are perduring processions then most of the ordinary persistence sentences that we take to be true are not true.
(16.5) Therefore, perduring processions are not sufficient for persistence.

Premise (16.1) is entailed by semantic processionism and premise (16.2) is very plausible. Premises (16.4) and (16.5) follow from other premises. So, the question is whether premise (16.3) is true. Why think it is true? One way to defend (16.3) is to consider *variation* across space. The rug in front of me is coloured red at one end and white at the other. Freddie the labradoodle has a head at one end and a tail at the other. This is variation across space. Objects vary across space by being composed of distinct spatial parts that have different properties: Freddie is composed of a head and a tail (and various other bits), which is why he varies across space. The rug is composed of red thread and white thread, which is why it varies across space.

We are not inclined to say that Freddie or the rug *change* over space (or so goes the thought). Rather, we are inclined to say that Freddie and the rug *vary* over space. What it is to vary over space is to have some spatial parts with certain properties, and other spatial parts with different properties. But, so the argument goes, change is not mere variation; change over time is not like variation over space. If change over time is different from variation across space, it must consist in something other than having different parts at different times with different properties. But according to the semantic processionist, perduring processions 'differ' across time by having temporal parts at different times with different properties. So perduring processions *vary* over time, but do not *change*. Hence (16.3) is true.[38] Now, one might deny that there is no change over space. One might maintain that things change both over time and over space. Even if that is right, though, it doesn't straightforwardly solve the problem since the objector might argue that change over time is quite *different* from change over space. In what follows I will talk as though there is *variation* over space and *change* over time, but nothing I say really hangs on this being so. My aim is just to show that the semantic processionist can accommodate these being relevantly different. I think she will want to do this even if she thinks they are both just kinds of change.

I think the semantic processionist has a fairly straightforward response to this argument. She can agree that there are differences between variation across space, on the one hand, and change over time, on the other. But she need not locate those differences in a difference in the way that objects are extended through time as opposed to space. Rather, she can locate the difference in a difference between the kinds of relations that obtain between the spatial

---

[38] The idea that change over time is incompatible with perdurance has been put forward by Klein (1999) (though Klein also thinks that endurance is incompatible with change over time), Hinchliff (1996), and Oderberg (2004). For arguments to the contrary see Johnson (2007) (although Johnson argues that our *experience* of change is compatible with perdurantism).

parts of an object at a given time, and the kinds of relations that obtain between an object at one time, and the object at another time.

Remember that for the semantic processionist persistence partly consists in the obtaining of gen-identity relations over time. If gen-identity relations turn out to be substantive dependence relations (such as existential dependence relations) then it turns out that change *propagates* along the temporal dimension because of the way in which the object later in time depends on the object earlier in time. The presence of this dependence means that often we can project forward in time to predict what objects will be like at later times. Indeed, part of what we are doing when we track persisting objects over time is making such predictions (imagine the way you track a dog at a dog park). Even if gen-identity does not involve such robust dependence relations, it is clear that they do involve us projecting along the temporal dimension. Our world does, at the very least, consist in certain sorts of projectible patterns that allow us to work out how matters will be at later times in virtue of how they were at earlier times, and which appear to allow us to intervene on later times, by intervening on earlier ones.

This means that change over time is quite different from mere spatial variation. We can rarely project 'sideways' across space: we can rarely predict the contents of one region by knowing what is in the contents of some spatially adjacent region.[39]

So, the reason change over time is different from variation across space has nothing to do with the way in which persisting objects are extended through time: it has nothing to do with whether they are extended through time by having temporal parts at different locations (by perduring) or by being multiply located (enduring). Rather, what explains the difference between change over time and spatial variation is the fact that objects persist along the temporal, but not the spatial, dimension and that persisting objects are ones that proceed, where procession necessarily involves the obtaining of gen-identity relations over time.

Viewed in this way, we can see that the semantic processionist has a *better* account of the difference between change over time and spatial variation. She thinks that it is the presence of these gen-identity relations that constitutes there being a persisting object. For she thinks that the essence of persistence is procession. So, for her, what it is to be a persisting thing is to be something that is quite

---

[39] Obviously sometimes we can do this. Sometimes this is because we already have some view about what exists in the larger region. I can predict that there will be a cushion and legs in this region by seeing there is a cushion and legs in that region, and forming the view that I am seeing part of a couch. These cases are clearly disanalogous since we have good predictive power in the temporal case even when we don't already know what will happen. In other cases, we can predict what will exist at one spatial region by knowing what exists at another. If a very large spatial region contains sand, then we might predict that regions adjoining it will also contain sand, and often we will be right. So it is not that we cannot ever predict what will occur at some spatial region, based on how things are at other regions. But our capacity to do so is more limited. Moreover, it is rare indeed that we can intervene on one spatial region by intervening on another.

different over time than it is over space. By contrast, insofar as semantic endurantists, perdurantists, and transdurantists allow that there can be enduring, perduring, or transduring objects that are not processions, they cannot think that it is the essence of persisting things to be different in this way across time and across space.

Consider, for instance, an enduring object that is not a procession. That object will be one that has the same sorts of properties and relations over time as it does over space: it will not change over time, but instead, will merely vary. That is because the way that an enduring object is at one time is irrelevant to how it is at other times; we cannot predict how/where it will be at later times based on how/where it is at earlier times; we cannot intervene on how it is at later times by intervening on how it is at earlier times, and so on.

What this tells us is that change over time is not, essentially, about how things are extended over time, but rather, about the relations that obtain between that object at different times. Since semantic processionists take persistence to consist precisely in these kinds of relations, they are very well placed to explain the difference between change and spatial variation: better placed, indeed, than their competitors.

To recap, then, in this section we considered an argument against semantic processionism that tried to show that perduring processions are not sufficient for persistence. The argument for this claim proceeded via the claim that perduring processions do not change, and hence that perduring processions cannot be sufficient for persistence. In response, I've argued that we should reject the claim that perduring processions do not change. Instead, I've suggested that change is intimately connection to procession, and hence that the semantic processionist has a better account of the difference between change and spatial variation than do her competitors.

In what follows I take up another objection to semantic processionism. This argument – the master argument: endurantist version – tries to show that *enduring* processions are not sufficient for persistence, and hence that semantic processionism is false.

5.2 Against the Persistence of Enduring Processions

Master Argument: Endurantist Version

(18) According to semantic processionism, the presence of enduring processions is sufficient for persistence.

(19) The presence of enduring processions is not sufficient for persistence.

(20) Therefore, semantic processionism is false.

The weight of the argument rests on premise (19). Why think (19) is true?

One suggestion is that objects, unlike properties, cannot be multiply located (Benovsky 2009). While we can find redness both here, and over there, by *that very redness* being multiply located, what it is to be an object is, *inter alia*, to be singly located. On one way of thinking of this worry, it's the worry that it is metaphysically impossible for objects to be multiply located because there simply are no worlds at which object-like things are multiply located. Another way of spelling out the worry is that given what we *mean* by 'object' they are the kinds of things that cannot be multiply located. So even if there could be object-like things that are multiply located, these wouldn't be *objects*. If the first of these is true, then enduring objects turn out to be impossible. That is no problem for the semantic processionist, since she does not claim that endurance is possible: she only claims that if there are enduring processions, then those things persist. If the second of these claims is true, though, then it does present a problem for the processionist. For she thinks that enduring processions persist; but if enduring processions are not even objects, then given that we are interested in *object persistence*, presumably it follows that they do not persist (qua objects).

The problem with this argument is that it's just not obvious that 'object' has a meaning which rules out multiply located things as being objects. To be sure, we don't expect to find objects multiply located at the same time (though notice that time travel might suggest otherwise) in the way we do properties. But if we have the intuition that in some good sense all of Annie is at t, and then all of her is also at t* (and so on) then this just seems to be another way of saying that she is multiply located: she's located at each of these times.

So this does not seem to be a good reason to endorse premise (19). Is there a better one? In what follows, I'll present the argument from temporary intrinsics and use this to try to motivate (19). I will then respond to the argument.

5.2.1 The Argument from Temporary Intrinsics

The first defence of (19) is an argument that is strictly analogous to the argument from change that we have already met, except that instances of 'perduring' have been replaced with 'enduring'. Here is that argument.

The Argument from Change, Redux

(19.1) Enduring processions are sufficient for persistence only if the presence of enduring processions makes true most of the ordinary persistence sentences that we take to be true (semantic processionism).

(19.2) Most of the ordinary persistence sentences that we take to be true are true only if ordinary objects change over time.

(19.3) If ordinary objects are enduring processions, then they do not change over time.

(19.4) Therefore, if ordinary objects are enduring processions, then most of the ordinary persistence sentences that we take to be true are not true.

(19.5) Therefore, enduring processions are not sufficient for persistence.

In this case the argument rests on premise (19.3). The argument from temporary intrinsics aims to show that (19.3) is true.

To make life easier, let's suppose that property P is incompatible with Q. (If it helps, imagine that P is the property of being red all over and Q is the property of being green all over. Then if something is P, it is not Q, and vice versa.)

The Argument from Temporary Intrinsics

(19.3.1) If O endures from t to t*, then there are two times, t and t*, which exist, such that O exists at each of them.

(19.3.2) An object genuinely changes only if there are some *intrinsic* properties, P and Q, such that O instantiates P at one time (t) and Q at another time (t*).

(19.3.3) Intrinsic properties are instantiated *simpliciter*.

(19.3.4) If O endures, then the only candidate to instantiate P and Q is O.

(19.3.5) O cannot both instantiate P and Q *simpliciter* (incompatibility of properties).

(19.3.6) If O instantiates P at t and Q at t*, then O does not instantiate P, *simpliciter*.

(19.3.7) Therefore, neither P nor Q is an intrinsic property of O.

(19.3.8) Therefore, O does not instantiate different intrinsic properties at different times.

(19.3.9) Therefore, O does not genuinely change.

Lewis (1986, 1988, 2002) offers an argument of this kind.[40]

Let's work our way through the argument from temporary intrinsics. Premise (19.3.1) says that if O endures through some interval that includes t and t*, then both of those times exist, and O exists at each of them. On the face of it this looks plausible. But I return to it shortly.

Premise (19.3.2) introduces the idea of genuine change. This is to be compared with Cambridge change, which is a merely relational change. Freddie is sitting next to me on the couch now. Shortly he will get up and wander into the kitchen. I will undergo a change from having the property of having Freddie sitting next to me, to having the property of having Freddie standing three

---

[40] Giberman (2017) more recently defends this argument.

metres away. But this is a merely relational change: nothing about me in myself changes. Genuine non-relational change occurs when my intrinsic properties change: when I am different in myself. Let's say that, very roughly, my intrinsic properties are the properties I have just in virtue of how I am, and not in virtue of how anything else is. We might say that they are the properties I would have if I were the only thing in a world (again very roughly). Properties such as mass, (but not weight) and shape are usually thought to be intrinsic. Given this, premise (19.3.2) seems plausible. Genuine change is characterised by a change in intrinsic properties rather than a change in Cambridge properties.

Premise (19.3.3) says that intrinsic properties are instantiated *simpliciter*. It's not always super clear what this means, either.[41] Roughly, though, the idea is that intrinsic properties are simply properties that I have, or lack. I do not have my shape relative to Freddie, or relative to a context, or relative to an observer. Notice that this is somewhat different to the idea that intrinsic properties are properties that I have, in myself. Suppose that Freddie is sitting next to me. Then I have the property of sitting next to Freddie. That property is not intrinsic in the sense that I have it, in myself, independent of how anything else is. But I do have that property *simpliciter* (or so we might think). It's not that I have that property relative to Freddie, or relative to some other observer. I simply have that property, although it's a property I can only have because of where Freddie is located.

Premise (19.3.4) is surely true. If O endures then what exists at one time (and is P) is O, and what exists at some other time and is Q, is also O: the only candidate to be the thing that instantiates P or Q is O itself. Premise (19.3.5) is also true. O cannot both instantiate P (*simpliciter*) and instantiate Q (*simpliciter*) on pain of contradiction. Nothing is both P and Q (given, remember, that we defined P and Q as incompatible properties).

So, since O exists at t and t*, and is P at one time and Q at another, it must be that O does not instantiate P or Q *simpliciter* (since otherwise this would result in contradiction). It must be that O instantiates each of P and Q *relative to a time*. Perhaps, instead of the instantiation relation being a two-place one that obtains between O and P, it obtains between O, P, and the time (t) and between O, Q, and the time (t*). So perhaps O is really P-at-t and Q-at-t* (Mellor 1981) or perhaps O is really at-t, P, and at-t* Q, (Johnston 1987) or perhaps O is P-tly and Q t*ly (Haslanger 1989; Ehring 1997).[42]

Regardless, it follows that neither P nor Q are intrinsic properties of O since intrinsic properties are instantiated *simpliciter*. Given this, O does not instanti-ate different intrinsic properties at different times, because it doesn't instantiate

---

[41] See Giberman (2017) for discussion of this issue.

[42] For discussion of these options see Eddon (2010a). For more on whether endurantists can make sense of the instantiation of properties, *simpliciter*, see Braddon-Mitchell and Miller (2007).

intrinsic properties at all. Hence O does not genuinely change. Since O is just an arbitrary object, it follows that if ordinary objects are enduring processions then they do not genuinely change over time, and (19.3) is true.

We could just as easily run the same argument, minimally amended, to reach conclusion (19.3*): if ordinary objects are transduring processions, then they do not genuinely change over time. We could then plug (19.3*) into a new argument that would aim to show that the presence of transduring processions is not sufficient for persistence, and hence provide an additional argument against semantic processionism. To get this conclusion, we just need to replace (19.3.4) in the argument above with (19.3.4*): if O transdures, then the only candidate to instantiate P and Q is O. Then we'd get the conclusion that if ordinary objects are transduring processions, they do not genuinely change over time.

It's easier to see why the argument from temporary intrinsics generalises to transduring objects if we ask ourselves why it is that a similar argument *doesn't* show that perduring processions do not genuinely change over time.

Remember that the perdurantist holds that objects are four-dimensional and that they change over time by having temporal parts with different properties. So, suppose that O is a perduring object. Then the analogue of (19.3.4) is not true. It's not the case that there is nothing other than O to be the bearer of P and Q. According to the perdurantist, there is a temporal part of O, TP, that is P, and another temporal part, TP*, that is Q. Each of these temporal parts simply instantiates P (or Q) *simpliciter*. There is, of course, no contradiction here, since TP is distinct from TP* (and of course two distinct things can be such that one is P, and the other is Q). Hence something has the property of being P, *simpliciter*, namely, TP, and something else has the property of being Q, *simpliciter*, namely, TP*, and O has those properties by having TP and TP* as temporal parts.[43]

It should now be clear why transduring processions also face the problem of temporary intrinsics. For transduring objects, too, lack temporal parts. So there is nothing other than the transduring thing itself to be the bearer of P and of Q.[44]

One response to the argument from temporary intrinsics is to deny (19.3.1). Presentists hold that only the present moment (and things) exist.[45] So, if O is P at t, and not at t*, there is no threat of incompatibility: for when t exists, it is simply the case that O is P. O at t* does not exist, and so there is no sense in which O is Q. *Mutatis mutandis* for when t* is present.[46]

---

[43] Lewis (1986) and Sider (2001).

[44] For discussion of this issue, see Parsons (2000) and Miller (2009).

[45] For explication and defence of presentist versions of the A-theory, see Crisp (2003); Bourne (2006); Tallant (2012); Ingram (2016, 2019); (Paoletti (2016); Deasy (2017); and Pezet (2017).

[46] Defenders of this way of responding to the problem of temporary intrinsics include Merricks (1994, 1999) and Pezet (2019).

The problem with this response is that presentism is itself a controversial view.[47] Moreover, one might think that presentism sits pretty uneasily with the existence of transduring processions.[48] Certainly the semantic processionist does not want to *have* to endorse presentism.

Moreover, there is a related argument, which I will call the argument from identity over time, that also aims to show that (19.3) is true. Endorsing presentism doesn't help to respond to that argument, so it's not a general solution.

The Argument from Identity over Time

(19.3.10) For any object O, O changes over time only if O has P at one time, and lacks P at some other time (necessary condition for change).

(19.3.11) If x=y then for all properties P, x has P iff y has P (the Indiscernibility of Identicals).

(19.3.12) For any object O, if O has P at t, and does not have P at t*, then O at t is numerically distinct from O at t*.

(19.3.13) Therefore, for any object O, O changes over time only if O does not endure (that is, changing objects do not endure).

(19.3.14) Therefore, if ordinary objects are enduring processions, then they do not change over time.

Let's work our way through the argument. Premise (19.3.10) is very plausible. It does not say that an object being one way at one time, and a different way at some other time, is *sufficient* for it to count as changing over time (after all, the properties in question might not be intrinsic ones, and so it might be mere Cambridge change). It simply says that an object *only* changes over time if it is one way at one time and another way at another time. It's hard to see how one could deny this: if the object is the same at each time, then surely it has not changed.

Premise (19.3.11) is what is known as the Indiscernibility of Identicals. The principle was formulated by Leibniz. It says that if x and y are identical, then for any property whatsoever, x has that property iff y does. That principle is widely accepted. The converse principle, which says that if x and y share all and only the same properties, then they are identical, is disputed. But we don't need that second principle here. The Indiscernibility of Identicals is surely true. If x=y then there is one thing, and 'x' and 'y' are two names for that thing.

---

[47] Problems associated with presentism include (but are not limited to) problems arising from special relativity, see Putnam (1967); Hinchliff (2000); and Balashov and Janssen (2007); and from truthmaking, see Keller (2004); Crisp (2007); Cameron (2008); Markosian (2012); Tallant (2013); and Tallant and Ingram (2015).

[48] Though see Brogaard (2000) for a defence of perdurantism in the context of presentism; similar considerations could be brought to bear here.

So, what 'x' picks out must have the same properties as what 'y' picks out, since they are picking out the same thing.

Premise (19.3.12) seems to follow from (19.3.10) and (19.3.11). Suppose we have O at t which has property P, and O* at t* which lacks P. Then there is some property (P) that O at t has, and O* at t* lacks. Hence it follows that O is not identical with O*.

Premise (19.3.13) follows from (19.3.12). If O changes then it cannot endure, for what it is to endure is to be numerically identical over time, and what it is to be numerically identical over time is to have the *same* properties over time; but what it is to change is to have *different* properties over time. Hence (19.3.14) follows: if ordinary objects are enduring processions then they do not change over time.

Endorsing presentism does not help us respond to this argument. Even if presentism is true, and it's the case that it is now t* and so O is Q, O now has the property of *having once not been* P (i.e., when O was P at t). Now of course, O can have the property of being Q, and of having once been P: these properties are not incompatible. But nevertheless, how can it be that O, as it was in the past, is numerically identical with O now, given that O *had* different properties from the properties that it now has?

How should the semantic processionist respond? Well, fortunately, endurantists have already done her work for her. A natural suggestion is that O has a single set of properties which are relativised to times. Suppose that O is P (at t) and Q (at t*). Then we can say that O has *both* P-at-t and Q-at-t* (for example). There is a single set of temporally relativised properties that O instantiates. So, in some good sense O *doesn't* change its properties. It always has the very same set of such properties. Still, O changes over time because the properties O has are temporally relativised, and which time it is changes. O has P-at-t at all times, but O only manifests being P when it is t, and not when it is t*: when it is t*, O manifests being Q. Notice that this is the very same sort of relativisation that was introduced in the argument from temporary intrinsics in order to avoid it being the case that O has incompatible properties. There, we said that O has P-at-t and has Q-at-t*. Even though O cannot be both P and Q *simpliciter*, it can be P-at-t and Q-at-t*.

The problem with this proposal, in the context of the argument from temporary intrinsics, is that change is supposed to involve a change in intrinsic properties. But on this view there are no truly intrinsic properties, because all properties are really in some sense disguised relations to times. O is never just straightforwardly P or Q, it is always P-at-t, or at-t, P (and so on). And defenders of the argument from temporary intrinsics argue that intrinsic properties are not like this. Shape and mass are not really relations to times.

What should we say in response to this? Certainly, it seems right to say that genuine change involves a change in intrinsic properties *in some good sense of intrinsic* as compared to mere Cambridge change. What is not clear, however, is whether or not the notion of intrinsic that is at play is one in which intrinsic properties cannot be in any sense relational. Indeed, further consideration seems to undermine that idea. Suppose that the sorts of properties involved in genuine change are relational properties, in that they are disguised relations to times. What distinguishes changes in these properties from changes in other relational properties that constitute mere Cambridge change? Well, it can still be the case that instantiating P is intrinsic in the sense that whether O has P at t depends solely on how O is, in and of itself at t, independently of anything else (Haslanger 1989). My property of sitting next to Freddie at t is not one I can instantiate independent of anything else at t: for I can only instantiate it given that Freddie is sitting next to me at t. By contrast, other properties (such as perhaps mass and shape) are ones that I can instantiate at t, independent of how anything else is at t. So, we can say that genuine change consists in a change of properties that an object instantiates independent of anything else at a time, while mere Cambridge change is a change in properties that an object instantiates depending on how something else is at the time. Then we can make good sense of the idea that enduring processions undergo genuine change.[49] So we have no reason to accept (19.3), and so no reason to conclude that enduring processions do not change, and hence that they do not persist.

Given this, we can reject these sorts of arguments against semantic processionism. If processions endure, then – some of them – genuinely change; if processions perdure, then – some of them – genuinely change.

Earlier in this Element I suggested that one reason to accept semantic processionism is that it provides an easy way of vindicating persistence realism. In the following section I argue for this claim.

6 Persistence Realism

Semantic processionism is a view on which if our world is, roughly, as it seems to us to be, then most of the ordinary persistence sentences we take to be true will turn out to be true. That is because if our world is as it seems to be then there are processions. Indeed, there are relevant processions: the right sorts of processions to make most of our persistence sentences true. And so, there being those things just guarantees that persistence realism is true.

Moreover, given semantic processionism we can tell that persistence error theory is false. First, we can determine that semantic processionism itself is true

---

[49] See Wasserman (2003) and Eddon (2010).

just by looking at our use of persistence sentences and the various scenarios in which we are inclined to say that something persists or does not. That is, we can tell that semantic processionism gives us the right way of spelling out the semantic claim. Second, we can easily determine that, conditional on semantic processionism being true, our persistence sentences are, by and large, true. That is because in order to ascertain whether those sentences are true, we don't first need to know any heavy-duty metaphysical facts about our world. We don't need to know whether the things around us endure (or perdure or transdure). All we need do is notice that we have P-experiences and that the fact that we have those experiences means that if things are as they seem to us to be, then there are processions. So, if things are as they seem to us to be, then persistence realism is vindicated.

Of course, semantic processionism does not *entail* that persistence realism is true. It could still turn out that things are not as they seem to us to be. Perhaps we are all suffering under a massive illusion. For instance, perhaps there is a single moment of time and so all of our P-experiences of there being other times are misleading. If so, our ordinary persistence sentences will not be true since there will be no processions. Persistence error theory will be vindicated. But in this eventuality, things are not as they seem to us to be. For it does not seem to us as though our world contains only a single moment of time.

So semantic processionism does not guarantee that persistence error theory is false; that is as one might hope: for there surely are some ways our world could turn out to be, in which persistence error theory would be true. Rather, it simply guarantees that if things are roughly as they seem to be, then persistence error theory is false.

Here is the argument for persistence realism from the truth of semantic processionism.

The Argument for Realism

(21) If our ordinary persistence sentences are mostly true, then persistence realism is true (definition of persistence realism).

(22) Our true ordinary persistence sentences are made true by the existence of (relevant) processions (semantic processionism).

(23) If our world is as it seems to us to be, then there exist (relevant) processions.

(24) Therefore, if our world is as it seems to us to be, then our ordinary persistence sentences are (mostly) true.

(25) Therefore, if our world is as it seems to us to be, then persistence realism is true.

Premise (21) is just a statement of persistence realism. Premise (22) is entailed by semantic processionism. Premises (24) and (25) follow from (21)–(23). So, the weight of the argument rests on (23). Much of what I have said so far in this Element speaks to why I think (23) is true. What it takes for there to be processions is just for there to be multiple M-regions whose contents either directly bear gen-identity relations to one another, or where there are chains of gen-identity relations between the contents of those M-regions. But I've said that gen-identity relations are just whatever relations it is that our P-experiences track, or which ground our having these P-experiences. Given that we have such experiences (which clearly we do), it is practically certain that there are gen-identity relations. Indeed, it is practically certain that if things are as they seem to us to be, then there exist the relevant processions to make true many or most of the ordinary persistence sentences that we take to be true. That is why we can tell that persistence realism is true: for we can tell that we have P-experiences and, barring our inhabiting a deeply sceptical world (such as one that contains no time), we can tell that things are as they seem to us to be. Hence, we can tell that there are processions and therefore that, mostly, the persistence sentences that we take to be true will in fact turn out to be true.

7 The Nature of Actual Processions

One thing that hopefully will have become clear by now is that arguments that are broadly in favour of, or against, a certain view of persistence are sometimes really arguments in favour of, or against, certain of the semantic theses I've been discussing. At other times, arguments are really arguments about what we should think of the actual nature of processions. It's important to keep these arguments separate since they are designed to target different questions.

In what follows, I consider some of the arguments that have been advanced, which are best thought of as giving us reason to think that actual processions have a particular underlying metaphysical nature.

Let's begin with the argument from prudential rationality. If sound, this argument doesn't tell us what underlying nature processions have; but it does tell us what nature they *don't* have: namely, they don't perdure.

The Argument from Prudential Rationality

(26) The axiom of prudence says that a person should promote his or her own overall welfare.

(27) If the axiom of prudence is true and actual persons perdure, then actual person-stage, P, is rationally required to promote the welfare of any person-stage, P*, that is a stage of the same person as P.[50]

(28) If P* is numerically distinct from P, then P* is not rationally required to promote the welfare of P.

(29) So if persons perdure, then the axiom of prudence is false.

(30) The axiom of prudence is not false.

(31) Therefore, persons do not perdure.

(32) Actual persons persist in the same manner as other actually persisting things.

(33) So if actual persons do not perdure, then no actual objects perdure.

(34) Therefore, no actual persisting objects perdure.[51]

The axiom of prudence says that a person should promote his or her own overall welfare. Let's suppose this is true, and that it's true regardless of whether the person desires to do so.[52] Premise (27) reframes the axiom of prudence in terms of perduring persons.

Why accept (28)? Well, it might seem that the presence of relations of numerical identity ground there being prudential reasons. Why should I, now, care about the welfare of my future self?: because that future self *is me*. Insofar as I care about myself, I must care about her. For she is me. Then it might seem plausible that in the absence of relations of numerical identity there can be no prudential reasons. Consider two temporal parts of a persisting person: me-now

---

[50] Strictly speaking the axiom of prudence says that P is rationally required to promote the overall welfare of person-stages, collectively, that are stages of the same person as P. This premise says something stronger than that. It seems plausible, though, that if P has reason to promote the overall welfare of all such stages collectively, then it has a *pro tanto* reason to promote the welfare of each of them singly.

[51] Arguments such as this are more often marshalled not just against perdurantist views of persistence, but more broadly against reductionist views of personal identity (the view on which personal identity reduces to the obtaining of certain mental and physical properties of person-stages, and the relations between said stages). Arguments of this kind have been considered (or defended) by, *inter alia*, Butler (1975), Parfit (1984), and Schechtman (1996, 2005, 2014). The dialectic here is a little murky. Sometimes these kinds of objections to reductionist views seem to simply suppose that reductionists must in fact be committed to something like perdurantism on the grounds that the continuity relations that reductionists appeal to clearly are not identity relations. Certainly, there are those who argue that endurantists cannot endorse reductionism precisely because identity does not reduce to, or consist in, the obtaining of these other relations (see, for instance, Merricks 1999). On the other hand, some reductionists clearly do seem to think that their view is consistent with strict identity over time (at least as long as the account includes a non-branching requirement), and take themselves to be giving an account of what that identity consists in (see, for instance, Parfit 1984). But if numerical identity over time in some sense consists in the obtaining of these kinds of continuity relations, then it's unclear why reductionists have any more of a problem than non-reductionists in explaining what grounds prudential rationality. At any rate, we are interested in this argument as it pertains to perdurantism, rather than as it pertains to reductionist views in general.

[52] See Parfit (1984) for a defence of this view.

and future-me. Me-now has to make a decision about whether to eat the chocolate cake or not. If me-now forgoes the chocolate cake so that future-me can have the cake, then I am depriving me-now of the cake in order that *someone else* gets to eat it. For, on this view, me-now is numerically distinct from future-me. But why should me-now do any such thing? Better, why should me-now have *prudential* reason to do so? Perhaps me-now might have *ethical* reasons to do so – me-now might forgo the cake in order that someone else, who is hungrier, can have the cake, and that someone else might be future-me – but me-now doesn't have prudential reasons to do so. But if so, there are no prudential reasons for me-now to care about the welfare of my future selves: I should care about them just insofar as I generally care about the welfare of others.[53]

Premises (29)–(31) follow from (26)–(28). Premise (32) strikes me as true.[54] We'd expect persons to persist in the same manner as other things. Of course, we'd expect the persistence conditions of persons to be different from the persistence conditions of tables or caterpillars. But it would be surprising if actual persons persisted by, say, enduring, and other things persisted by perduring. Premises (33) and (34) follow from earlier premises.

Remember, even if this argument is sound it doesn't show that semantic processionism is false; it just shows that we should think that actual processions do not perdure. But in fact, I don't think this is a good argument. Moreover, considering why it fails will be instructive in revealing yet another reason why we should find semantic processionism to be an attractive view.

The reason I think the argument fails is because I think that (28) is false. I'll argue that it's the fact that me-now and future-me are members of the same procession that grounds the former having prudential reason to care

---

[53] There are other arguments, sometimes pitched as arguments against perdurantism, which appeal to normative (prudential and moral) considerations pertaining to persons. Those arguments aim to show that because perdurantists are committed to there being many short-lived person-like objects (all the extended temporal parts/person-stages of persons which are not the whole persons), she faces difficulties. There is a cluster of such arguments, which aim to show that the existence of these person-like objects (what Olson (2010) calls sub-persons and Johnston (2017a, 2017b) calls personites) is normatively problematic. The idea is that these things have the same moral standing as persons (since they are intrinsically just like persons). But those things are often punished for events that happened before they came into existence and make sacrifices whose benefit they will never see (because they will have ceased to exist before the benefit is accrued). While this argument is sometimes framed as an argument against perdurantism (and we might think of it as an argument to the conclusion that actual objects do not perdure) it is really (as Olson 2010 makes clear) a problem for any view on which there are such short-lived person-like objects: any view on which there is what is sometimes known as a profligate or generous ontology. Such views are not limited to perdurantist views: endurantists can accept that there exist multiple overlapping enduring things (for views of this kind, see Miller 2006). Given this, I won't consider such arguments here. For discussion of the general problem that such objects raise, see also Kaiserman (2019) and Eklund (2020).

[54] See Miller (2010) for arguments to the contrary.

about the welfare of the latter. Thus, it's not relations of numerical identity that ground prudential rationality (nor is it the relation of being-part-of-the-same-four-dimensional-whole.) Thus (28) is false: the axiom of prudence will be true as long as actual persons proceed; since there can be processions that perdure, it follows that the axiom of prudence can be true and yet persons perdure.

Let's start by imagining that relations of numerical identity can, and do, come apart from the existence of processions. Imagine two processions. The first we will call Hannah, and the second Allan. Hannah and Allan look like regular persisting persons. Hannah-at-t_5 remembers what happened to Hannah-at-t_4, and Hannah-at-t_5 counterfactually depends on Hannah-at-t_4. Hannah-at-t_4 deliberates about what she should do, and it is Hannah-at-t_5 that acts on the output of those deliberations. Likewise for Allan. In this regard, Hannah and Allan are just like you and me.

Now suppose that numerical identity 'jumps around' from procession to procession. Suppose that as a matter of fact, Hannah-at-t_2 is numerically identical with Allan-at-t_3, who is numerically identical with Hannah-at-t_4, who is numerically identical with Allan-at-t_5, and so on. Likewise, Hannah-at-t_1 is numerically identical with Allan-at-t_2, who is numerically identical with Hannah-at-t_3, and so on. So we have two enduring objects, each of which is always a person-at-a-time.

Does Hannah-at-t_2 have prudential reason to promote the welfare of Allan-at-t_3, and no such reason to promote the welfare of Hannah-at-t_3? Well, Hannah-at-t_3 is not numerically identical with Hannah-at-t_2 and is numerically identical with Allan-at-t_3. So, if relations of numerical identity are what matter when it comes to grounding prudential reason, then this is exactly what we should think. I doubt, however, that we judge that Hannah-at-t_2 has prudential reason to promote the welfare of Allan-at-t_3 and no prudential reason to promote the welfare of Hannah-at-t_3.

If Hannah-at-t_2 is given the choice between Hannah-at-t_3 and Allan-at-t_3 suffering a painful toothache, I say she has prudential reason to prefer that Allan-at-t_3 has the toothache. Allan-at-t_3 has no memories of what Hannah-at-t_2 did, nor does he share any of her beliefs, projects, values, or motivations. Hannah-at-t_2 does have prudential reason to promote the welfare of Hannah-at-t_3. After all, Hannah-at-t_3 has the beliefs, desires, and projects that she does because of the beliefs, desires, and projects of Hannah-at-t_2. Hannah-at-t_2 is too short-lived to act on the output of her deliberations, or to bring her projects to fruition. But she knows that Hannah-at-t_3 is well placed to do so: she knows in fact, that the output of her own deliberations will causally affect Hannah-at-t_3 in such a way that she *will* act on those deliberations. Hannah-at-t_3 is, in effect, Hannha-at-t_2's agent in the world: she is the thing that will enact Hannah-at-t_2's decisions and bring her projects to fruition.

If you share my intuitions in these cases, this tells us that the presence of relations of numerical identity does not, on its own, ground prudential rationality.

Of course, the endurantist might argue that endurance entails procession, and so the case I just described is impossible. I've already argued that it's not clear that we should accept this claim. But I don't need to make that case here. For we can develop the same worry without supposing that facts about numerical identity over time can 'jump around' between processions.

Parfit (1984) has already made this case by appealing to fission. Suppose that teletransportation preserves personal identity. In the ordinary run of things, when Mary gets into the teletransportation machine, she survives and exits the machine in a different location. Suppose Mary is told, as she steps into the machine, that the person who gets out the other end will be abducted and tortured, but that by paying $100 now, she can avoid this. We presumably all agree that Mary has a prudential reason to pay the money. Now suppose that fission occurs, such that two persons step out of the machine at the other end. The two persons – A1 and A2 – who step out of the machine are both equally psychologically and physically continuous with the person, Mary, who entered the machine.

Parfit (1984) thinks, and I agree, that Mary has reason to promote the welfare of both A1 and A2. If one, or both, of them will be abducted and tortured, and if Mary can avoid this by paying $100, then it seems that she has just as much reason to pay the $100 in this case as she did in the previous one.

It cannot be, however, that Mary is numerically identical with both A1 and A2, unless A1 and A3 are identical with one another. Identity is transitive. If x is identical with y, and y is identical with z, then x is identical with z. So, if Mary is numerically identical with both A1 and A2, then A1 and A2 are numerically identical with one another. If that were true then Mary would be multiply located *at the same times*. Although this view has been defended as a way of thinking about what is going on in cases of fission (see Miller 2006), most people deny that A1 and A2 are identical, and hence deny that Mary is identical with either of them.

In that case either just one of A1 and A2 is numerically identical with Mary, or neither is. Since both A1 and A2 bear the same non-identity involving relations to Mary (such as psychological and physical continuity), philosophers who are *reductionists* about personal identity (that is, who think that personal identity reduces to facts about the psychological and physical properties of persons-stages, and the relations between them)[55] conclude that neither is identical to Mary. So, if Mary endures, then fission marks the cessation of her persistence.[56] Yet it seems that Mary should promote the well-being of both A1 and A2. On the basis of reasoning such as this, Parfit concludes that what matters in survival is not identity at all. For, he reasons, Mary clearly does have prudential reasons to care about A1 and A2, even though she is not identical with either.

I think that the right conclusion to draw here is that what grounds prudential rationality is not numerical identity: rather, what grounds it is the nature of the connections between persons at times – in particular, the fact that a person at one time is gen-identity related to a person at another time (or there is a chain of such relations connecting the two). That is just to say that it is because persons proceed that a person at one time has reason to promote the welfare of that person at another time. They have such reasons if they proceed by enduring, but equally, they have those reasons if they proceed by perduring (or succeeding). And this just gives us further reason to think that semantic processionism is the right way of spelling out the semantic claim.

In addition, it tells us that we should reject the argument from prudential rationality. Perhaps actual processions do not perdure, but this argument does not give us reason to think that this is so.

That brings us to another argument, which aims to show that actual persisting objects do not endure.

The Argument from Coincidence

(35) Actual ordinary numerically distinct objects cannot be exactly located at the same region.

(36) Actual ordinary persisting objects coincide at times.

(37) If actual ordinary persisting objects endure, then cases of coincidence at a time are cases in which numerically distinct objects are exactly located at the same region.

(38) Therefore, actual ordinary persisting objects do not endure.

This argument is often presented as a reason to think that actual processions perdure,[57] though as framed it only tells us (if sound) that such objects do not endure.

---

[55] Reductionists about personal identity include psychological continuity theorists, bodily continuity theorists, and animalists.

[56] So called non-branching views of reductionism hold this.

[57] Those who defend versions of this argument include Heller (1984, 2000); Hawley (2001); and Sider (2001).

Premise (35) is plausible. If ordinary object O is exactly located at R, then ordinary object O* cannot also be exactly located at R. Perhaps this is not true of weird objects. Perhaps ghosts and some particles are not like this; but toasters, dogs, and cars seem to be. When an ordinary object tries to move into a region occupied by another, it will push the other object out.

Ordinary persisting objects do coincide at some times. Consider a lump of clay and the statue made from the clay. There are times at which the two objects coincide. That is, there are times at which the clay and the statue are located at the same place.[58] So (36) is true.

Now suppose that the statue and the clay are enduring objects. Consider a time, t, at which they coincide. Since enduring objects are exactly located at each M-region (and hence at each time) it follows that at t, the statue is exactly located at some region, R, and that the clay is also exactly located at that same region. So (37) is true. Premise (38) follows from the other premises.[59]

This argument gives us reason to think that actual processions do not endure.

Does the argument generalise to other ways in which ordinary objects might persist? No. The analogous version of premise (37) is not true on any of the other views. To see this, suppose that actual ordinary objects perdure. Now consider the statue and the clay, which coincide at t. If the statue and the clay perdure, then it doesn't follow from the fact that they coincide at t that there exist two numerically distinct objects exactly located at the same region (R). That is because if the statue and the clay perdure, then there is only one object exactly located at R: namely, a momentary object which is a temporal part of both the perduring object that is the statue and the perduring object that is the clay. Coincidence at a time is, for the perdurantist, a matter of two distinct four-dimensional objects overlapping.[60] As such, the perdurantist is not committed to there being two objects exactly located at R.

There are several other similar sorts of 'puzzles' that can be parlayed into arguments in favour of the claim that actual objects persist in some particular manner. These include puzzles of grounding,[61] in which we worry about what could ground two coinciding objects having different modal properties at

---

[58] See Gilmore (2007).

[59] For discussion of this argument, see Eddon (2010b), Gilmore (2007), and Moyer (2009).

[60] See Lewis (1986) and Sider (2001). Of course, there are cases in which it looks like two objects coincide at all times, such as presented by Gibbard (1975) in which a statue and lump come into existence at the very same time and pass from existence at the same time. But typically, perdurantists hold that there is a single object present, which has two sets of counterparts (statue ones and lump ones), and that is why we attribute to it different modal properties and why it seems to us as though there are two things present when there are not (see, for instance, Sider 2001).

[61] This terminology is from Bennett (2004).

a particular time, given that at that time they are made up of exactly the same matter.[62]

As it happens, I think that the puzzles of coincidence give us *some* reason to think that actual processions do not endure. But I leave it to the reader to evaluate these arguments.

Other arguments reach the same conclusion by inviting us to imagine enduring objects in worlds with time travel. Imagine an enduring brick, which we repeatedly send back in time and use to build a wall. Given that the brick endures, the wall is composed of the *very same brick* many times over. That falls foul of certain fairly intuitive mereological principles, such as the principle that if P is a proper part of O, then O has some other proper part, x, which is distinct from P. That is because in this case the brick is a proper part of the wall (or at least, certainly appears to be), and yet the wall has no other proper parts that are distinct from the brick.[63] If it is successful, this argument would show not only that *actual* persisting objects do not endure, but also that, *necessarily*, objects do not endure. After all, mereological principles presumably hold of necessity (that is, in every world). So, suppose it is necessary that if P is a proper part of O, then O has some other proper part, x, which is distinct from P. Now suppose there is a possible world in which enduring objects time travel. If there were such a world, then there would be a world in which it is not true that if P is a proper part of O, then O has some other proper part, x, which is distinct from P. Hence, there can be no possible world in which enduring things time travel.

It seems very unlikely that it is the *combination* of endurance and time travel that is impossible. So, if one thinks that time travel is possible (as many philosophers do) then one will have to conclude that endurance is impossible. Hence, since necessarily objects do not endure, they do not actually endure. Of course, this argument can be resisted either by rejecting the idea that time travel is possible or by rejecting the mereological principle in question. So, it is controversial whether this shows us that endurance is impossible, and hence not actual.

Finally, there are various arguments that try to show that actual objects perdure (or at least, do not endure) which appeal to the phenomenon of vagueness.[64] These arguments take a number of forms. Very roughly, the central idea begins with the thought that composition itself is not vague. It's not a vague matter whether some xs compose something or not. That is because (or so the thought goes) *existence* is not vague. It cannot be vague whether or not y exists,

---

[62] See, for instance, Moyer (2009) for discussion of these issues.

[63] See Effingham and Robson (2007) and Daniels (2013, 2014(a), 2014(b)). For broader discussion of the idea that multi-location is paradoxical, see Barker and Dowe (2003, 2005).

[64] Lewis (1986) and Sider (2001, 2003) are the initial proponents of such arguments.

and so it cannot be vague whether or not some xs compose something (i.e., y). (Although, of course, it can be vague whether the xs compose a table as opposed to, say, something that is table-like but not a table.)

Now consider an ordinary persisting thing. Let's take a dog – Freddie – as our example. It seems to be a vague matter at *exactly* which moment Freddie ceases to exist. The perdurantist can accommodate this being so. For she can say that there are many overlapping four-dimensional dog-like objects each of which goes out of existence at a slightly different time. Each of these objects is perfectly precise in its temporal boundaries. None of these objects is in any way vague. The reason it seems to us to be a vague matter at exactly which moment Freddie ceases to exist is because it is a vague matter exactly *which* of these precise objects is Freddie (or, if you prefer, vague which object the name 'Freddie' picks out). So, the vagueness is merely semantic. All of the objects are perfectly precise, and we locate the vagueness in imprecision about which of these objects ordinary names pick out.

By contrast, the thought goes, the endurantist has to locate the vagueness in the world. For the endurantist does not think that there exist multiple overlapping dog-like things. She thinks there is a single thing that is Freddie. But if it's a vague matter when Freddie goes out of existence, then it must be a vague matter whether, at certain times, Freddie exists or not. Since it is never a vague matter whether something exists or not, it cannot be that Freddie endures.

There has been a good deal of discussion of arguments such as these.[65] The supposition underlying this kind of argument is that perdurantists are committed to there being a large ontology of overlapping persisting objects and endurantists are committed to denying this claim. But this claim about ontology really has nothing to do with endurantism and perdurantism. The endurantist can adopt a generous ontology in which there exist various overlapping enduring objects.[66] So, she can respond to the argument from vagueness in much the same way as the perdurantist, by holding that the vagueness in question is merely a semantic matter. Of course, as a matter of fact many endurantists do not adopt a generous ontology: but the general point here is that these two arguments rest on ontological claims that are not essential to any view of persistence, and so neither provide us with a decisive reason to think that actual objects endure, or that they perdure.

That concludes my discussion of some of the more common arguments that purport to give us reason to think that actual objects persist in one, or another, manner.

---

[65] Discussion can be found in Koslicki (2003), Lowe (2005), and Miller (2005, 2008).

[66] For an example of such a view, see Miller (2006b, 2008). For discussion, see also Magidor (2016).

8 Conclusion

My aim, in this Element, has been to do three things: first, to argue for persistence realism; second, to argue for semantic processionism; and third, to clearly distinguish between arguments that speak to the issue of what persistence is – what our world needs to be like for there to be persisting things, and in particular, for most of our ordinary persistence sentences to be true – and the issue of how it is that actual objects in fact persist.

I've argued that one reason to endorse semantic processionism is that it gives us an easy route to persistence realism. It is a view on which if things are, roughly, as they seem to us to be then there are persisting things, and those things make (most of) our ordinary persistence sentences true. If semantic processionism is true, then it's easy to see how we can be confident that persistence realism is true. By contrast, if other views are true, then it's not clear that we can be confident that persistence realism is true (even if it is). Having resolved the semantic question, however, we do not thereby resolve the substantive underlying metaphysical question about the nature of actual processions. Thus, we need to carefully distinguish between the sorts of arguments we might marshal in favour of, say, semantic processionism, and those we might marshal in favour of a particular conclusion about the underlying nature of processions.

References

Armstrong, D. M. (1980). 'Identity through Time', in P. van Inwagen (ed.), *Time and Cause*. D. Reidel, pp. 67–78.

Balashov, Y. (2000a). 'Persistence and Space–Time: Philosophical Lessons of the Pole and Barn'. *The Monist* 83(3): 321–340.

Balashov, Y. (2000b). 'Relativity and Persistence'. *Philosophy of Science* 67(3): 549–62.

Balashov, Y. (2000c). 'Enduring and Perduring Objects in Minkowski Space–Time'. *Philosophical Studies* 99: 129–66.

Balashov, Y. and Janssen, M. (2003). 'Presentism and Relativity'. *British Journal for the Philosophy of Science* 54(2): 327–46.

Bardon, A. (2013). *A Brief History of the Philosophy of Time*. Oxford University Press.

Barker, S. and Dowe, P. (2003). 'Paradoxes of Multi-Location'. *Analysis* 63: 106–114.

Barker, S. and Dowe. P. (2005). 'Endurance Is Paradoxical'. *Analysis* 65: 69–74.

Bennett, K. (2004). 'Spatio-Temporal Coincidence and the Grounding Problem'. *Philosophical Studies* 118(3): 339–71.

Benovsky, J. (2009). 'On (Not) Being in Two Places at the Same Time: An Argument against Endurantism'. *American Philosophical Quarterly* 46(3): 239–48.

Bourne, C. (2006). *A Future for Presentism*. Oxford University Press.

Braddon-Mitchell, D. (2004). 'Masters of Our Meanings'. *Philosophical Studies* 118(1–2): 133–52.

Braddon-Mitchell, D. (2009). 'Naturalistic Analysis and the A Priori', in D. Braddon-Mitchell and R. Nola (eds.), *Conceptual Analysis and Philosophical Naturalism*. MIT Press, pp. 349–61.

Braddon-Mitchell, D. and Miller, K. (2006). 'Talking about a Universalist World'. *Philosophical Studies* 130(3): 507–42. https://doi.org/10.1007/s11098-004-5752-6.

Braddon-Mitchell, D. and Miller, K. (2007). 'There Is No Simpliciter'. *Philosophical Studies* 136(2): 249–78. https://doi.org/10.1007/s11098-007-9074-3.

Braddon-Mitchell, D. and Nola, R. (eds.) (2009). *Conceptual Analysis and Philosophical Naturalism*. MIT Press.

Brogaard, B. (2000). 'Presentist Four-Dimensionalism'. *The Monist* 83(3): 341–56.

Brower, J. E. (2010). 'Aristotelian Endurantism: A New Solution to the Problem of Temporary Intrinsics'. *Mind* 119(476): 883–905.

Butler, J. (1975). 'Of Personal Identity', first appendix to *The Analogy of Religion*. In J. Perry (ed.), *Personal Identity*. University of California Press, pp. 99–105. First published in 1736.

Cameron, R. (2008). 'How to Be a Truthmaker Maximalist'. *Noûs* 42: 410–21.

Chalmers, D. (2004). 'Epistemic Two-Dimensional Semantics'. *Philosophical Studies* 118: 153–226.

Chalmers, D. J. and Jackson, F. (2001). 'Conceptual Analysis and Reductive Explanation'. *Philosophical Review* 110(3): 315–61.

Chisholm, R. (1976). *Person and Object: A Metaphysical Study*. Open Court.

Contessa, G. (2014). 'One's a Crowd: Mereological Nihilism without Ordinary-Object Eliminativism'. *Analytic Philosophy* 55 (2): 199–221.

Correia, F. (2005). *Existential Dependence and Cognate Notions*. Philosophica Verlag.

Costa, D. (2017). 'The Transcendentist Theory of Persistence'. *Journal of Philosophy* 114(2): 57–75.

Costa, D. and Giordani, A. (2016). 'In Defence of Transcendentism'. *Acta Analytica* 31(2): 225–34.

Crisp, T. (2003). 'Presentism', in M. J. Loux and D. W. Zimmerman (eds.), *The Oxford Handbook of Metaphysics*. Oxford University Press, pp. 211–46.

Crisp, T. M. (2007). 'Presentism and the Grounding Objection'. *Noûs* 41(1): 90–109.

Daniels, P. (2013). 'Endurantism and Paradox'. *Philosophia* 41(4): 1173–79.

Daniels, P. (2014a). 'Occupy Wall: A Mereological Puzzle and the Burdens of Endurantism'. *Australasian Journal of Philosophy* 92(1): 91–101.

Daniels, P. (2014b). 'The Persistent Time Traveller: Contemporary Issues in the Metaphysics of Time and Persistence'. PhD thesis, Monash University.

Daniels, P. (2019). 'Persistence, Temporal Extension, and Transdurantism'. *Metaphysica* 20(1): 83–102.

Deasy, D. (2017). 'What Is Presentism'. *Noûs* 51(2): 378–97.

Deng, N. (2013a). 'Fine's McTaggart, Temporal Passage, and the A versus B-Debate', *Ratio* 26(1): 19–34.

Deng, N. (2013b). 'Our Experience of Passage on the B-Theory', *Erkenntnis* 78 (4): 713–26.

Deng, N. (2019). 'One Thing After Another: Why the Passage of Time Is Not an Illusion', in A. Bardon, V. Arstila, S. Power, and A. Vatakis (eds.), *The Illusions of Time: Philosophical and Psychological Essays on Timing and Time Perception*. Palgrave Macmillan, pp. 3–17.

Devitt, M. (1991). *Realism and Truth*. Blackwell.

Dowe, P. (2009). 'Causal Process Theories', in H. Beebee, C. Hitchcock, and P. Menzies (eds.), *The Oxford Handbook of Causation*. Oxford University Press, pp. 213–34.

Eagle, A. (2010a). 'Perdurance and Location', in D. Zimmerman (ed.), *Oxford Studies in Metaphysics: Volume 5*. Oxford University Press, pp. 53–94.

Eagle, A. (2010b). 'Duration in Relativistic Spacetime', in D. Zimmerman (ed.), *Oxford Studies in Metaphysics: Volume 5*. Oxford University Press, pp. 113–17.

Eddon, M. (2010a). 'Three Arguments from Temporary Intrinsics'. *Philosophy and Phenomenological Research* 81(3): 605–19.

Eddon, M. (2010b). 'Why Four-Dimensionalism Explains Coincidence'. *Australasian Journal of Philosophy* 88(4): 721–28.

Effingham, N. and Robson, J. (2007). 'A Mereological Challenge to Endurantism'. *Australasian Journal of Philosophy* 85(4): 633–40.

Ehring, D. (1997). *Causation and Persistence: A Theory of Causation*. Oxford University Press.

Eklund, M. (2020), 'The Existence of Personites'. *Philosophical Studies* 177: 2051–71.

Farr, M. (2012). Towards a C Theory of Time: An Appraisal of the Physics and Metaphysics of Time Direction. PhD thesis, University of Bristol.

Farr, M. (2020). 'C-Theories of Time: On the Adirectionality of Time'. *Philosophy Compass* 12(1): 1–17.

Gibbard, A. (1975). 'Contingent Identity'. *Journal of Philosophical Logic* 4(2): 187–222.

Giberman, D. (2017). 'Bent Not Broken: Why Exemplification Simpliciter Remains a Problem for Eternalist Endurantism'. *Erkenntnis* 82(5): 947–66.

Gilmore, C. (2007) 'Time Travel, Coinciding Objects, and Persistence', in D. Zimmerman (ed.), *Oxford Studies in Metaphysics: Volume 3*. Oxford University Press, pp. 177–98.

Giordani, A. and Costa, D. (2013). 'From Times to Worlds and Back Again: A Transcendentist Theory of Persistence'. *Thought: A Journal of Philosophy* 2(1): 210–20.

Hales, S. and Johnson, T. (2003). 'Endurantism, Perdurantism and Special Relativity'. *Philosophical Quarterly* 53(213): 524–39.

Haslanger, S. (1989). 'Endurance and Temporary Intrinsics'. *Analysis* 49: 119–25.

Hawley, K. (2001). *How Things Persist*. Oxford University Press.

Hawley, K. (2020). 'Temporal Parts', in E. Zalta (ed.), *The Stanford Encyclopedia of Philosophy*, Summer edition. https://plato.stanford.edu/entries/temporal-parts/.

Heller, M. (1984). Hunks: An Ontology of Physical Objects. PhD thesis, Syracuse University.

Heller, M. (1990). *The Ontology of Physical Objects*. Cambridge University Press.

Heller, M. (2000). 'Temporal Overlap Is Not Coincidence'. *The Monist* 83(3): 362–80.

Hinchliff, M. (1996). 'The Puzzle of Change'. *Philosophical Perspectives* 10: 119–36.

Hinchliff, M. (2000). 'A Defense of Presentism in a Relativistic Setting'. *Philosophy of Science* 67(3): 586.

Hudson, H. (2001). *A Materialist Metaphysics of the Human Person*. Cornell University Press.

Ingram, D. (2016). 'The Virtues of Thisness Presentism'. *Philosophical Studies* 173(11): 2867–88.

Ingram, D. (2019). *Thisness Presentism: An Essay on Time, Truth, and Ontology*. Routledge.

Ismael, J. (2012). 'Decision and the Open Future', in A. Bardon (ed.), *The Future of the Philosophy of Time*. Routledge, pp. 149–69.

Ismael, J. (2017). 'Passage, Flow, and the Logic of Temporal Perspectives', in C. Bouton and P. Huneman (eds.), *Time of Nature and the Nature of Time*. Springer Verlag, pp. 23–39.

Jackson, F. (1998a). 'Reference and Description Revisited'. *Philosophical Perspectives* 12: 201–18.

Jackson, F. (1998b). *From Metaphysics to Ethics*. Oxford University Press.

Jackson, F. (2004). 'Why We Need A-Intensions'. *Philosophical Studies* 118: 257–77.

Jackson. F. (2007). 'Reference and Description from the Descriptivists' Corner', *Philosophical Books* 48(1): 17–26.

Jackson, F. (2009). 'A Priori Biconditionals and Metaphysics', in D. Braddon-Mitchell and R. Nola (eds.), *Conceptual Analysis and Philosophical Naturalism*. MIT Press, pp. 99–113.

Johnson, T. A. (2007). 'Time for Change'. *Southern Journal of Philosophy* 45 (4): 497–513.

Johnston, M. (1983). Particulars and Persistence. PhD thesis, Princeton University. https://philpapers.org/archive/JOHPAP-15.pdf.

Johnston, M. (1987). 'Is There a Problem about Persistence?'. *Proceedings of the Aristotelian Society* 61(supplement): 107–35.

Johnston, M. (2017a). 'The Personite Problem: Should Practical Reason Be Tabled?'. *Noûs* 51: 617–44.

Johnston, M. (2017b). 'Personites, Maximality, and Ontological Trash'. *Philosophical Perspectives* 30: 198–228.

Kaiserman, A. (2019). 'Stage Theory and the Personite Problem'. *Analysis* 79: 215–22.

Keller, S. (2004) 'Presentism and Truthmaking' in D. Zimmerman (ed.), *Oxford Studies in Metaphysics: Volume 1*. Oxford University Press, pp. 83–104.

King, J. (2001). *Complex Demonstratives: A Quantificational Approach*. MIT Press.

Klein, C. J. (1999). 'Change and Temporal Movement'. *American Philosophical Quarterly* 36(3): 225–39.

Koslicki, K. (2003). 'The Crooked Path from Vagueness to Four-Dimensionalism'. *Philosophical Studies* 114: 107–34.

Kripke, S. (1980). *Naming and Necessity*. Harvard University Press.

Kroon, R. (1987). 'Causal Descriptivism'. *Australasian Journal of Philosophy* 65(1): 1–17. https://doi.org/10.1080/00048408712342731.

Le Poidevin, R. (1991). *Change, Cause and Contradiction: A Defence of the Tenseless Theory of Time*. St. Martin's Press.

Leininger, L. J. (2013). B-Coming: Time's Passage in the B-Theory Blockworld. PhD Thesis, College Park, University of Maryland.

Leininger, L. (2018). 'Objective Becoming: In Search of A-Ness.' *Analysis* 78 (1): 108–17. 10.1093/analys/anx155.

Leininger, L. (2021). 'Temporal B-Coming: Passage without Presentness'. *Australasian Journal of Philosophy* 99(1): 1–17.

Lewin, K. (1922). *Der Begriff der Genese in Physik, Biologie und Entwicklungsgeschichte*. Springer.

Lewis, D. (1976). 'Survival and identity', in A. O. Rorty (ed.), *The Identities of Persons*. University of California Press.

Lewis, D. (1984). 'Putnam's Paradox'. *Australasian Journal of Philosophy* 62: 221–36.

Lewis, D. (1986). *On the Plurality of Worlds*. Wiley-Blackwell.

Lewis, D. (1988). 'Rearrangement of Particles: Reply to Lowe. *Analysis* 48(2): 65–72.

Lewis, D. (1999). *Papers in Metaphysics and Epistemology*. Cambridge University Press.

Lewis, D. (2002). 'Tensing the Copula.' *Mind* 111(441): 1–14.

Loar, B. (1976). 'The Semantics of Singular Terms'. *Philosophical Studies* 30: 353–77.

Longenecker, M. T.-S. (2020). 'Perdurantism, Fecklessness and the Veil of Ignorance'. *Philosophical Studies* 177: 2565–76.

Longenecker, M. T.-S. (2021). 'Is Consequentialist Perdurantism in Moral Trouble?'. *Synthese* 198: 10979–90. https://doi.org/10.1007/s11229-020-02764-3.

Lowe, E. J. (1987). 'Lewis on Perdurance versus Endurance'. *Analysis* 47(3): 152–54.

Lowe, E. J. (1994). 'Ontological Dependency'. *Philosophical Papers* 23(1): 31–48.

Lowe, E. J. (2005). 'Vagueness and Endurance'. *Analysis* 65: 104–12.

Lowe, E. J. (2013). 'Some Varieties of Metaphysical Dependence', in M. Hoeltje, B. Schnieder, and A. Steinberg (eds.), *Varieties of Dependence: Ontological Dependence, Grounding, Supervenience, Response-Dependence*. Philosophia, pp. 193–210.

Magidor, O. (2016). '"Endurantism vs Perdurantism": A Debate Reconsidered'. *Noûs* 50(3): 509–32.

Markosian, N. (2008). 'Restricted Composition', in T. Sider, J. Hawthorne, and D. W. Zimmerman (eds.), *Contemporary Debates in Metaphysics*. Blackwell, pp. 341–63.

Markosian, N. (2012). 'The Truth about the Past and Future', in F. Correia and A. Iacona (eds.), *Around the Tree: Semantic and Metaphysical Issues concerning Branching and the Open Future*. Springer, pp 2127–41.

Maudlin, T. (2007). *The Metaphysics within Physics*. Clarendon Press.

McCall, S. and Lowe, D. J. (2002). '3D/4D Equivalence, the Twins Paradox and Absolute Time'. *Analysis* 63(2): 114–23.

Mellor, D. H. (1981). *Real Time*. Cambridge University Press.

Mellor, D. H. (1998). *Real Time II*. Taylor & Francis.

Merricks, T. (1994). 'Endurance and Indiscernibility'. *Journal of Philosophy* 91 (4): 165–84.

Merricks, T. (1999a). 'Persistence, Parts, and Presentism'. *Noûs* 33(3): 421–38.

Merricks, T. (1999b). 'Endurance, Psychological Continuity, and the Importance of Personal Identity'. *Philosophy and Phenomenological Research* 59(4): 983–97.

Merricks, T. (2001). *Objects and Persons*. Oxford University Press.

Miller, K. (2004). 'Enduring Special Relativity'. *Southern Journal of Philosophy* 42(3): 349–70.

Miller, K. (2005a). 'The Metaphysical Equivalence of Three and Four Dimensionalism'. *Erkenntnis* 62(1): 91–117.

Miller, K. (2005b) 'Blocking the Path from Vagueness to Four Dimensionalism'. *Ratio* 18(3): 317–31. https://doi.org/10.1111/j.1467-9329.2005.00293.x.

Miller, K. (2005c). 'What Is Metaphysical Equivalence?'. *Philosophical Papers* 34(1): 35–74. https://doi.org/10.1080/05568640509485150.

Miller, K. (2006a). 'Travelling in Time: How to Wholly Exist in Two Places at the Same Time'. *Canadian Journal of Philosophy* 36(3): 309–34. https://doi.org/10.1353/cjp.2006.0019.

Miller, K. (2006b): 'Non-Mereological Universalism'. *European Journal of Philosophy* 14(3): 404–22.

Miller, K. (2008). 'Endurantism, Diachronic Vagueness and the Problem of the Many'. *Pacific Philosophical Quarterly* 89(2): 242–53.

Miller, K. (2009). 'Ought a Four-Dimensionalist to Believe in Temporal Parts?'. *Canadian Journal of Philosophy* 39(4): 619–46.

Miller, K. (2010). 'Persons as Sui Generis Kinds: Advice to Exceptionists'. *Philosophy and Phenomenological Research* 81(3): 567–94. https://doi.org/10.1111/j.1933-1592.2010.00379.x.

Miller, K. (2013). 'Times, Worlds and Locations'. *Thought* (Special Issue: The Metaphysics of Time and Modality) 2(3): 221–27. https://doi.org/10.1002/tht3.86.

Miller, K. (2017). 'A Hyperintensional Account of Metaphysical Equivalence'. *Philosophical Quarterly* 67(269): 772–93.

Moyer, M. (2009). 'Does Four-Dimensionalism Explain Coincidence?'. *Australasian Journal of Philosophy* 87: 479–88.

Noonan, H. (1993). 'Constitution Is identity'. *Mind* 102: 133–46.

Oaklander, L. N. (2012). 'A-, B-, and R-Theories of Time: A Debate', in A. Bardon (ed.), *The Future of the Philosophy of Time*. Routledge, pp. 1–24.

Oderberg, D. S. (2004). 'Temporal Parts and the Possibility of Change'. *Philosophy and Phenomenological Research* 69(3): 686–708.

Olson, E. T. (2010). 'Ethics and the Generous Ontology'. *Theoretical Medicine and Bioethics* 31: 259–70.

Paoletti, M. P. (2016). 'A Sketch of (an Actually Serious) Meinongian Presentism'. *Metaphysica* 17(1): 1–18.

Parfit, D. (1984). *Reasons and Persons*. Oxford University Press.

Parsons, J. (2000). 'Must a Four-Dimensionalist Believe in Temporal Parts?'. *The Monist* 83(3): 399–418.

Parsons, J. (2007). 'Theories of Location', in D. Zimmerman (ed.), *Oxford Studies in Metaphysics: Volume 3*. Oxford University Press, pp. 201–32.

Parsons, J. (2008). 'Hudson on Location'. *Philosophy and Phenomenological Research* 76: 427–35.

Parsons, J. (2013). 'Conceptual Conservatism and Contingent Composition'. *Inquiry: An Interdisciplinary Journal of Philosophy* 56(4): 327–39.

Parsons, J. (2015). 'A Phenomenological Argument for Stage Theory'. *Analysis* 75(2): 237–42.

Pezet, R. E. (2017). 'A Foundation for Presentism'. *Synthese* 194(5): 1809–37.

Pezet, R. (2019). 'An Explanatory Virtue for Endurantist Presentism'. *Philosophia* 47(1): 157–82.

Price, H. (1996). *Time's Arrow and Archimedes' Point: New Directions for the Physics of Time*. Oxford University Press.

Prosser, S. (2012). 'Why Does Time Seem to Pass?'. *Philosophy and Phenomenological Research* 85(1): 92–116.

Putnam, H. (1967). 'Time and Physical Geometry'. *Journal of Philosophy* 64: 240–7.

Quine, W. V. (1950). 'Identity, Ostension, and Hypostasis'. *Journal of Philosophy* 47: 621–33.

Rea, M. (1998). 'Temporal Parts Unmotivated'. *Philosophical Review* 107(2): 225–60.

Rettler, B. (2018). 'Mereological Nihilism and Puzzles about Material Objects'. *Pacific Philosophical Quarterly* 99(4): 842–68.

Rychter, P. (2012). 'Stage Theory and Proper Names'. *Philosophical Studies* 161(3): 367–79.

Salmon, N. (1981). *Reference and Essence*. Princeton University Press.

Salmon, N. (1983). *Frege's Puzzle*. MIT Press.

Salmon, W. (1994). 'Causality without Counterfactuals'. *Philosophy of Science* 61(2): 297–312.

Savitt, S. F. (2002). 'On Absolute Becoming and the Myth of Passage'. *Royal Institute of Philosophy Supplements* 50(1): 153–67.

Schechtman, M. (1996). *The Constitution of Selves*. Cornell University Press.

Schechtman, M. (2005). 'Experience, Agency, and Personal Identity'. *Social Philosophy and Policy* 22(2): 1–24.

Schechtman, M. (2014). *Staying Alive: Personal Identity, Practical Concerns, and the Unity of Life*. Oxford University Press.

Shumener, E. (2020). 'Explaining Identity and Distinctness'. *Philosophical Studies* 177(7): 2073–96.

Sider, T. (1993). 'van Inwagen and the Possibility of Gunk'. *Analysis* 53: 285–9. *Institute of Philosophy Supplements* 50(1): 153–67.

Sider, T. (1996). 'All the World's a Stage'. *Australasian Journal of Philosophy* 74(3): 433–53.

Sider, T. (2000). 'The Stage View and Temporary Intrinsics'. *Analysis* 60(1): 84–8.

Sider, T. (2001). *Four Dimensionalism*. Clarendon Press.

Sider, T. (2003). 'Against Vague Existence'. *Philosophical Studies* 114: 135–46.

Sider, T. (2013). 'Against Parthood', in K. Bennett and D. Zimmerman (eds.), *Oxford Studies in Metaphysics: Volume 8*. Oxford University Press, pp. 237–93.

Simons, P. (1985). 'Coincidence of Things of a Kind'. *Mind* 94: 70–5.

Soames, S. (1987). 'Direct Reference, Propositional Attitudes, and Semantic Content'. *Philosophical Topics*,15(1): 47–87.

Soames, S. (2002). *Beyond Rigidity: The Unfinished Semantic Agenda of Naming and Necessity.* Oxford University Press.

Soames, S. (2004). 'Reference and Description', in F. Jackson and M. Smith (eds.), *The Oxford Handbook of Contemporary Analytic Philosophy.* Oxford University Press, p. 397.

Tallant, J. (2012). '(Existence) Presentism and the A-theory'. *Analysis* 72(4): 673–81.

Tallant, J. (2013). 'Dubious by Nature'. *Canadian Journal of Philosophy* 43: 97–116.

Tallant, J. (2014). 'Against Mereological Nihilism'. *Synthese* 191(7): 1511–27.

Tallant, J. and Ingram, D. (2015). 'Nefarious Presentism'. *Philosophical Quarterly* 65: 355–71.

Thomson, J. J. (1983). 'Parthood and Identity Across Time'. *Journal of Philosophy* 80: 201–20.

Thomson, J. J. (1998). 'The Statue and the Clay'. *Nous* 32: 149–73.

van Inwagen, P. (1990a). *Material Beings.* Cornell University Press.

van Inwagen, P. (1990b). 'Four-Dimensional Objects'. *Nous* 24: 245–55.

Varzi, A. C. (2003). 'Perdurantism, Universalism and Quantifiers' *Australasian Journal of Philosophy* 82(2): 208–14.

Velleman, J. D. (2006). 'So It Goes'. Amherst Lecture in Philosophy.

Wahlberg, T. H. (2014). 'The Endurance/Perdurance Controversy Is No Storm in a Teacup'. *Axiomathes* 24(4): 463–82.

Wasserman, R. (2003). 'The Argument from Temporary Intrinsics'. *Australasian Journal of Philosophy* 81(3): 413–19.

Wasserman, R. (2016). 'Theories of Persistence'. *Philosophical Studies* 173: 243–50.

Yablo, S. (2001). 'Go Figure: A Path through Fictionalism'. *Midwest Studies in Philosophy* 25(1): 72–102.

Cambridge Elements

Metaphysics

Tuomas E. Tahko

University of Bristol

Tuomas E. Tahko is Professor of Metaphysics of Science at the University of Bristol,
UK. Tahko specializes in contemporary analytic metaphysics, with an emphasis on
methodological and epistemic issues: 'meta-metaphysics'. He also works at the
interface of metaphysics and philosophy of science: 'metaphysics of science'. Tahko is the
author of *Unity of Science* (CUP, 2021, *Elements in Philosophy of Science*),
An Introduction to Metametaphysics (CUP, 2015) and editor of *Contemporary
Aristotelian Metaphysics* (CUP, 2012).

About the Series

This highly accessible series of Elements provides brief but comprehensive introductions
to the most central topics in metaphysics. Many of the Elements also go into
considerable depth, so the series will appeal to both students and academics. Some
Elements bridge the gaps between metaphysics, philosophy of science, and
epistemology.

Cambridge Elements ☰

Metaphysics

Elements in the Series

Printed in the United States
by Baker & Taylor Publisher Services